GRADE 6

Common Core Language

M000276590

Table of Contents

Introduction

What Is the Common Core?

The Common Core State Standards are an initiative by states to set shared, consistent, and clear criteria for what students are expected to learn. This helps teachers and parents know what they need to do to help students. The standards are designed to be rigorous and pertinent to the real world. They reflect the knowledge and skills that young people need for success in college and careers.

If you teach in a state that has joined the Common Core State Standards Initiative, then you are required to incorporate these standards into your lesson plans. Students need targeted practice in order to meet grade-level standards and expectations, and thereby be promoted to the next grade.

What Does the Common Core Say About Language Standards?

In order for students to be college and career ready in language, they must gain control over many conventions of standard English grammar, usage, and mechanics as well as learn other ways to use language to convey meaning effectively.

Research shows that it is effective to use students' writing as a tool to integrate grammar practice. However, it is often hard to find a suitable context in which to teach such specific grade-level standards. Some students will need additional, explicit practice of certain skills. The mini-lessons and practice pages in this book will help them get the practice they need so they can apply the required skills during independent writing and on standardized assessments.

Students must also be proficient in vocabulary acquisition skills. This means being able to determine or clarify the meaning of grade-appropriate words. It also means being able to appreciate that words have nonliteral meanings, shades of meaning, and relationships to other words. These skills will enable students to read and comprehend rigorous informational texts and complex literary texts.

The Common Core State Standards state that the "inclusion of Language standards in their own strand should not be taken as an indication that skills related to conventions, effective language use, and vocabulary are unimportant to reading, writing, speaking, and listening; indeed, they are inseparable from such contexts."

Using This Book

Mini-Lessons and Practice Pages

Each grade-level volume in this series addresses all of the language standards for that grade. For each standard, three types of resources are provided that scaffold students using a gradual release model.

Based on your observations of students' language in writing and in collaborative conversations, choose mini-lessons that address their needs. The mini-lessons can be used during your literacy and writing block. Then use the practice pages to reinforce skills.

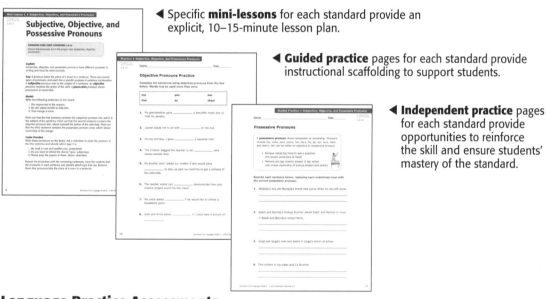

◀ Specific **mini-lessons** for each standard provide an explicit, 10–15-minute lesson plan.

◀ **Guided practice** pages for each standard provide instructional scaffolding to support students.

◀ **Independent practice** pages for each standard provide opportunities to reinforce the skill and ensure students' mastery of the standard.

Language Practice Assessments

Easy-to-use, flexible practice assessments for both Conventions and Vocabulary standards are provided in the last section of the book. The self-contained 2-page assessments cover skills in a reading passage format and have multiple choice answers.

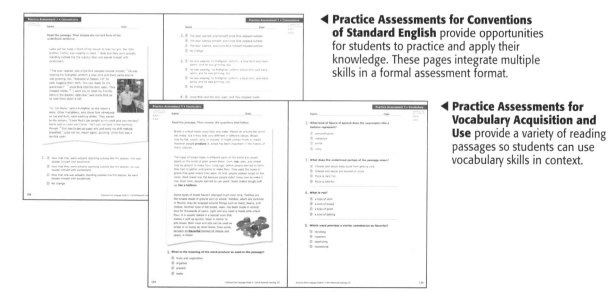

◀ **Practice Assessments for Conventions of Standard English** provide opportunities for students to practice and apply their knowledge. These pages integrate multiple skills in a formal assessment format.

◀ **Practice Assessments for Vocabulary Acquisition and Use** provide a variety of reading passages so students can use vocabulary skills in context.

Lesson Plan Teacher Worksheet

Conventions of Standard English and Knowledge of Language

The lessons in this section are organized in the same order as the Common Core Language Standards for conventions. Each mini-lesson provides specific, explicit instruction for a Language standard and is followed by multiple practice pages. Use the following chart to track the standards students have practiced. You may wish to revisit mini-lesson and practice pages a second time for spiral review.

Common Core State Standards	Mini-Lessons and Practice	Page	Complete (✓)	Review (✓)
L.6.1a	Mini-Lesson 1: Subjective, Objective, and Possessive Pronouns	6		
	Practice: Subjective Pronouns	7		
	Practice: Objective Pronouns	9		
	Practice: Possessive Pronouns	11		
L.6.1b	Mini-Lesson 2: Intensive Pronouns	14		
	Practice: Intensive Pronouns	15		
L.6.1c	Mini-Lesson 3: Pronoun Number and Person	18		
	Practice: Pronoun Number and Person	19		
L.6.1d	Mini-Lesson 4: Vague Pronouns	22		
	Practice: Vague Pronouns	23		
L.6.1e	Mini-Lesson 5: Standard English	26		
	Practice: Standard English	27		

(Conventions continued)

Common Core State Standards	Mini-Lessons and Practice	Page	Complete (✓)	Review (✓)
L.6.2a	Mini-Lesson 6: Use Punctuation (Commas, Parentheses, and Dashes) to Set Off Elements	32		
	Practice: Use Commas to Set Off Elements	33		
	Practice: Use Parentheses to Set Off Elements	35		
	Practice: Use Dashes to Set Off Elements	37		
L.6.2b	Mini-Lesson 7: Spell Correctly	40		
	Practice: Spell Correctly	41		
L.6.3a	Mini-Lesson 8: Vary Sentences for Meaning, Interest, and Style	44		
	Practice: Vary Sentences for Meaning	45		
	Practice: Vary Sentences for Interest	47		
	Practice: Vary Sentences for Style	49		
L.6.3b	Mini-Lesson 9: Maintain Consistency in Style and Tone	52		
	Practice: Maintain Consistency in Style	53		
	Practice: Maintain Consistency in Tone	55		

COMMON CORE
STATE STANDARD

L.6.1a

Subjective, Objective, and Possessive Pronouns

COMMON CORE STATE STANDARD L.6.1a
Ensure that pronouns are in the proper case (subjective, objective, possessive).

Explain

Subjective, objective, and possessive pronouns have different purposes in writing and must be used correctly.

Say: *A pronoun takes the place of a noun in a sentence. There are several types of pronouns, and each has a specific purpose in sentence construction. A **subjective** pronoun acts as the subject of a sentence. An **objective** pronoun receives the action of the verb. A **possessive** pronoun shows possession or ownership.*

Model

Write the following sentences on the board:

1. *She responded to the request.*
2. *Mr. Bin asked Jonelle to help him.*
3. *That mango is mine.*

Point out that the first sentence contains the subjective pronoun *she*, which is the subject of the sentence. Point out that the second sentence contains the objective pronoun *him*, which received the action of the verb *help*. Point out that the third sentence contains the possessive pronoun *mine*, which shows ownership of the mango.

Guide Practice

Write these sentences on the board. Ask a volunteer to circle the pronoun in the first sentence and identify which type it is.

1. *My neck is sore and swollen.* (my; possessive)
2. *Do you want to attend the dinner?* (you; subjective)
3. *Please pass the papers to them.* (them; objective)

Repeat the procedure with the remaining sentences. Have the students find the pronouns in each sentence and identify which type they are. Remind them that pronouns take the place of a noun in a sentence.

Common Core Language Grade 6 • ©2014 Newmark Learning, LLC

Name_____ Date_____

Common Core
State Standard
L.6.1a

Subjective Pronouns

> A **subjective pronoun** acts as the subject of a sentence and takes the place of a noun. Pronouns include *I, you, she, he, it, we,* and *they. You* and *it* can also be objective pronouns. Look for clues in sentences to help determine which pronoun to use.
>
> - Marvin asked his mother if <u>he</u> could go to the football game. (*he* replaces *Marvin*)
> - We waited for the bus, but <u>it</u> never arrived. (*it* replaces *bus*)

Read each sentence and underline the subjective pronouns.

1. I am going to attend the ballet with <u>my</u> mom and aunt.

2. Susie and her lab partner needed more time to finish the experiment, so <u>they</u> asked the teacher for an extension.

3. Phil practiced pitching during the summer because <u>he</u> wanted to try out for the baseball team.

4. My sister and I asked our father if <u>we</u> could have a sleepover this weekend.

5. Can <u>you</u> please write the equation on the board?

6. Peter went on adventures with his friends, and <u>they</u> always had fun.

COMMON CORE
STATE STANDARD

L.6.1a

Name_____ Date_____

Subjective Pronouns

Complete the sentences using subjective pronouns from the box below. Words may be used more than once.

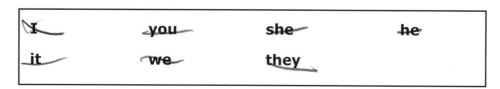

I	you	she	he
it	we	they	

1. Mr. Parnel arrived at the warehouse, but ___he___ did not have a key to unlock the doors.

2. Marcy received a flu vaccination so ___she___ will not get sick with the flu.

3. Sharon and William got married, and then ___they___ went on a honeymoon.

4. Josie and ___I___ asked our father if ___we___ could go to the park.

5. Will ___you___ please sign for the parcel when ___it___ arrives?

6. Maggie likes alfalfa, but ___she___ does not like corn.

7. Their mother asked if ___we___ would finish folding the laundry for her.

8. Would ___you___ like to go to the dance with me?

Name_____ Date_____

COMMON CORE
STATE STANDARD
L.6.1a

Objective Pronouns

An **objective pronoun** receives the action of the verb. Pronouns include *me, you, her, him, it, us,* and *them. You* and *it* can also be subjective pronouns, and *her* can also be a possessive pronoun.

- Theo, please don't interrupt <u>her</u>.
  (*her* is the object of *interrupt*)
- Jorge would like to talk to <u>you</u>.
  (*you* is the object of *talk*)

Read each sentence and circle the objective pronoun(s).

1. Would you like to come with me to the rodeo?

2. Excuse me, will you please give it to her?

3. Mrs. Walters knew them because they were in her class two years ago.

4. Ask him if he would like to attend the show with us.

5. Will you please move to the end of the line with them?

6. Your grandfather gave me his watch.

7. Rick played a song for me on his guitar.

8. Pamela showed us the beautiful painting she made.

COMMON CORE
STATE STANDARD
L.6.1a

Name_____ Date_____

Objective Pronouns Practice

Complete the sentences using objective pronouns from the box below. Words may be used more than once.

me	you	her
him	us	them

1. My grandmother gave _____me_____ a beautiful music box to hold my jewelry.

2. Lauren asked me to sit with _____her_____ on the bus.

3. For his birthday, I gave _____him_____ a baseball mitt.

4. The children begged the teacher to let _____them_____ take recess outside later.

5. My brother and I asked our mother if she would allow _____us_____ to stay up past our bedtime to get a glimpse of the asteroids.

6. Will the teacher ask _____you_____ to demonstrate for the class how your science project works?

7. His uncle asked _____him_____ if he would like to attend a basketball game.

8. Judy and Arnie asked _____you_____ if I could take a picture of _____us_____.

Common Core Language Grade 6 • ©2014 Newmark Learning, LLC

Name_____ Date_____

Common Core
State Standard
L.6.1a

Possessive Pronouns

> A **possessive pronoun** shows possession or ownership. Pronouns
> include *my, mine, your, yours, her, hers, his, its, our, ours, their,*
> and *theirs. Her* can be either an objective or possessive pronoun.
>
> - Enrique raised <u>his</u> hand to ask a question.
>   (*his* shows ownership of *hand*)
> - Marlene put <u>her</u> science project in <u>her</u> locker.
>   (*her* shows ownership of *science project* and *locker*)

**Rewrite each sentence below, replacing each underlined noun with
the correct possessive pronoun.**

1. <u>Michelle's</u> dog ate <u>Michelle's</u> brand new purse when he was left alone.

   Michelle's dog ate her brand new purse when he was left alone.

2. <u>Ralph and Bernito's</u> biology teacher asked Ralph and Bernito to hand
   in <u>Ralph and Bernito's</u> assignments.

   Their biology teacher asked Ralph & Bernito to hand in their assignments.

3. Jorge put <u>Jorge's</u> coat and books in <u>Jorge's</u> locker at school.

   Jorge put his coat & books in his locker at scholl.

4. This picture is <u>my sister and I's</u> favorite.

   This picture is our favorite.

COMMON CORE
STATE STANDARD

L.6.1a

Name_____ Date_____

Possessive Pronouns

Circle the correct possessive pronoun that completes each sentence.

1. Did you enter _____ poem in the poetry contest?

   a. your

   b. mine

2. Would you like to come to _____ house after school?

   a. theirs

   b. my

3. The referees made _____ decision about the play.

   a. their

   b. theirs

4. Roberto and I just bought a car. It is _____.

   a. my

   b. ours

5. Is this _____ binder?

   a. its

   b. your

6. Amir gave _____ apple to Judith.

   a. his

   b. hers

Name_____ Date_____

COMMON CORE STATE STANDARD L.6.1a

Subjective, Objective, and Possessive Pronouns

Write a brief paragraph correctly using at least two subjective pronouns, two objective pronouns, and two possessive pronouns. Underline each pronoun.

Did <u>you</u> know that Mary-Anns favorite place is the Turtleback beach. If <u>she</u> could <u>she</u> would spend night and day at the beach. <u>Her</u> favorite time to go is 4ᵗʰ of July fireworks at peak moon. <u>Mine</u> is at sunset, what is <u>yours</u>?

COMMON CORE
STATE STANDARD
L.6.1b

Intensive Pronouns

> **COMMON CORE STATE STANDARD L.6.1b**
> Use intensive pronouns (e.g., *myself*, *ourselves*).

Explain
Intensive pronouns emphasize the antecedent, or the word to which the pronoun refers, in writing.

Say: *Different types of pronouns have specific purposes in sentence construction and make writing enjoyable and easy to understand. An intensive pronoun emphasizes the antecedent, or the noun or pronoun to which the intensive pronoun refers, in a sentence. Examples of intensive pronouns include* myself, yourself, herself, himself, itself, yourselves, ourselves, *and* themselves.

Model
Write the following sentences on the board:

1. *He himself believed he would become a better tennis player.*
2. *We would like to build the shelves ourselves.*

Point out that the first sentence contains the intensive pronoun *himself*, which refers to the antecedent *he*. Point out that the second sentence contains the intensive pronoun *ourselves*, which refers to the antecedent *we*.

Guide Practice
Write the following sentences on the board. Ask a volunteer to underline the intensive pronoun and circle the antecedent in the first sentence.

1. *I myself am allowed to walk to school.* (underline *myself*; circle *I*)
2. *They paid the bill themselves.* (underline *themselves*; circle *they*)

Ask: *Were you able to find the intensive pronoun* myself *and recognize* I *as the antecedent in the first sentence?*

Repeat the procedure with the remaining sentence. Have the students find the intensive pronoun and antecedent. Remind students that intensive pronouns are used for emphasis and are not necessary to the meaning of the sentence.

Name_____ Date_____

COMMON CORE
STATE STANDARD
L.6.1b

Intensive Pronouns

An **intensive pronoun** emphasizes the antecedent in a sentence, or the word to which the pronoun refers. Intensive pronouns include *myself, yourself, herself, himself, itself, yourselves, ourselves,* and *themselves*.

- They <u>themselves</u> sat in the corner.
- Erin is going to visit the college <u>herself</u>.

Read each sentence and circle the intensive pronouns.

1. Nina designed the dress for the bride herself.

2. My father himself paid for the movie tickets for us.

3. We painted our neighbor's fence ourselves.

4. The players themselves are the heart and soul of the team.

5. The puppies learned to roll over themselves.

6. She herself needed a moment to catch her breath.

7. Did he paint the portrait himself?

8. I chopped the vegetables myself.

COMMON CORE
STATE STANDARD

L.6.1b

Name_____ Date_____

Intensive Pronouns

Complete the sentences using intensive pronouns from the box.

myself	yourself	herself	himself
itself	yourselves	ourselves	themselves

1. Lindsay embroidered the silk pillow _____.

2. I completed the enormous puzzle all by

    _____.

3. We have to make dinner _____.

4. The canary opened the cage door _____ and
    flew away.

5. The little boy helped _____ to some candy.

6. Can all of you please arrange the party _____?

7. They completed the chores _____.

8. You ate the whole pan of muffins all by

    _____?

Common Core
State Standard
L.6.1b

Name_____ Date_____

Intensive Pronouns

Complete the sentences using the correct intensive pronouns.

1. The judges selected the winner _____.
   a. himself
   b. themselves

2. Aunt Helen let us choose the movie we wanted to watch
   _____.
   a. ourselves
   b. yourselves

3. I _____ am going right to bed when I get
   home because I am exhausted.
   a. myself
   b. yourself

4. The lizard _____ changes color to deceive its
   potential enemies.
   a. themselves
   b. itself

5. Becky baked the cake for the birthday party
   _____.
   a. himself
   b. herself

6. My cousin Belinda _____ made the intricate
   sculpture located in the park.
   a. myself
   b. herself

COMMON CORE
STATE STANDARD
L.6.1c

Pronoun Number and Person

> **COMMON CORE STATE STANDARD L.6.1c**
> Recognize and correct inappropriate shifts in pronoun number and person.

Explain

Pronouns refer to a certain number (singular or plural) and a certain person (first, second, or third).

Say: *You already know that the different types of pronouns have specific purposes in sentence construction and make our writing enjoyable and easy to understand. Every pronoun refers to a certain number (singular or plural) and a certain person (first, second, or third). Writers should not shift the number and person within a sentence or paragraph.*

Model

Write the following sentences on the board:

1. *The students worked hard to earn money for his team.*
2. *Marla asked if we could spend the night at Joanie's house.*

Point out that the first sentence contains a number error. The incorrect pronoun *his* is singular and refers to the plural antecedent students. *His* should be changed to the plural pronoun *their*. The second sentence contains a number and person error. The incorrect pronoun *we* is plural and first-person, but it refers to the antecedent *Marla*, which is singular and third-person. We should be changed to the singular, third person pronoun *she*.

Guide Practice

Write the following sentences on the board. Ask a volunteer to underline the incorrect pronoun and replace it with the correct pronoun in the first sentence.

1. *Mrs. Bennett asked the students to model our experiments.* (underline *our*; correct answer: *their*)
2. *The boss asked Mr. Greene to prove its leadership skills.* (underline *its*; correct answer: *his*)

Repeat the procedure with the remaining sentence. Have the students correct the pronoun. Remind them that pronouns should always match in number and person.

COMMON CORE
STATE STANDARD
L.6.1c

Name_____ Date_____

Pronoun Number and Person

> **Pronouns** refer to a certain **number** (singular or plural) and a certain **person** (first, second, or third) in writing. Writers should not shift the number and person within a sentence or paragraph.
>
> The pronouns *you, your,* and *yours* can be either singular or plural depending on whether the writer or speaker is addressing one person or more than one.
>
> - If a student feels ill, <u>he</u> or <u>she</u> must visit the nurse's office.
> - The Boy Scouts earned badges for <u>their</u> hard work.

**Read each sentence and underline the incorrect pronoun(s).
Then write the correct pronoun(s) in the space provided.**

1. The black bear prepared themselves to hibernate all winter long.

   _____

2. The agitated dog broke free from our leash, and

   we darted under a bush in the neighbor's yard.

   _____

3. The wet, soapy plate slipped out of my hand and onto the floor,

   but she did not shatter. _____

4. If Aunt Sue calls, please ask him if you would like to come over

   for dinner tomorrow. _____

5. Saul gave the forecast to the viewers watching the news report

   on your televisions. _____

Common Core
State Standard

L.6.1c

Name_____ Date_____

Pronoun Number and Person

Complete the sentences using correct pronoun(s) from the box below.
Some pronouns may be used more than once and some not at all.

I	me	my	mine	myself
we	us	our	ours	ourselves
you	your	yours	yourself	she
her	hers	herself	he	him
his	himself	it	its	itself
they	them	their	theirs	themselves

1. My friends and I visited the museum where _____
   saw famous paintings such as *Starry Night.*

2. Amelia befriended the new boy and gave _____ a
   tour of the school.

3. After you are finished using the paint, make sure to put
   _____ lid back on tightly so _____
   won't dry out.

4. Autumn is my favorite time of year because the trees shed
   _____ brilliant leaves.

5. "You kids should watch where _____ are going!"
   shouted the man at the skateboarders.

6. The woman yelled at _____ employee over the
   incident.

7. Mr. Johnson told the students, "Please bring _____
   textbooks to class tomorrow so _____ can use them
   for the procedure.

8. I _____ dissolved the chemical in the solution
   during the experiment.

Name_____ Date_____

COMMON CORE
STATE STANDARD
L.6.1c

Pronoun Number and Person

Read each sentence and circle the correct pronoun(s).

1. Everyone should have received (his or her, their) bus assignments in the mail.

2. The team debuted (our, its) new uniforms at the homecoming game.

3. Bobby and Mary met the president of the university (himself, yourself).

4. The bay lamb groomed (my, its) matted fleece.

5. The spices are so old that (it, they) have lost most of (its, their) potency.

6. The nurse applied ointment to the wound so (they, it) would heal properly.

7. The baby squirrels cuddled with (her, their) mother for warmth in the sun.

8. *I wonder if I turned off the coffee pot,* Mrs. Flay thought to (yourself, herself).

9. Catherine and I visited (our, we) grandfather by (myself, ourselves) at his condo in Florida.

10. Andrea was late for school because (you, she) missed the bus.

COMMON CORE
STATE STANDARD
L.6.1d

Vague Pronouns

COMMON CORE STATE STANDARD L.6.1d
Recognize and correct vague pronouns (i.e., ones with unclear or ambiguous antecedents)

Explain
Pronouns must have clear and recognizable antecedents.

Say: *Different types of pronouns have specific purposes in sentence construction and make writing enjoyable and easy to understand. A pronoun emphasizes an antecedent, a noun, or a pronoun to which the pronoun refers, in a sentence. A pronoun and its antecedent must match, or agree, in number and person. If readers have difficulty identifying the antecedent in a sentence, or if there is no antecedent, then the sentence needs to be revised.*

Model
Write these sentences on the board:

1. *My mom drove Phyllis home after she finished grocery shopping.*
2. *After Phyllis finished grocery shopping, my mom drove her home.*

Point out that the first sentence contains the vague pronoun *she*, which leaves readers with the question "Who is grocery shopping?" Point out that a simple revision fixes the vague pronoun. Readers now know Phyllis was the person who was grocery shopping.

Guide Practice
Write the following sentence on the board. Ask a volunteer to underline the vague pronoun.

Yin told her sister that she really liked her new car. (underline the second *her*)
(sample answers: Yin said she really likes her sister's new car. Yin said to her sister, "I really like your new car.")

Have the students revise the sentence. Then have students revise the sentence again in a different way. Remind them that each pronoun should have a clear and recognizable antecedent.

Name_____ Date_____

COMMON CORE
STATE STANDARD
L.6.1d

Vague Pronouns

> A pronoun and its antecedent must agree. If readers have difficulty identifying the antecedent in a sentence because the **pronoun** is **vague**, then the sentence needs to be revised.
>
> - *Although the car backed into the fence, <u>it</u> was not damaged.*
>   (The pronoun *it* is vague, which causes us to ask the question, "What was not damaged?")
> - *The car, which backed into the fence, was not damaged.*
>   (A sentence revision clears up the vagueness of the sentence.)

Read each sentence and circle the vague pronoun(s).

1. The bag contained a pencil, book, and it was red.

2. Frank told his dad that his bike had a flat tire.

3. Take the box from the cabinet and close it.

4. The boss told the employee that he would receive a raise.

5. The neighbors invited their friends to the movies, but they didn't show up.

6. Marlene told Ariana that she liked her braided hair.

7. As she was placing the lid on the cookie jar, she dropped it to the floor.

8. Nigel and Hannah told Asa they would see them later.

Common Core
State Standard
L.6.1d

Name_____ Date_____

Vague Pronouns

Read each sentence and underline the vague pronoun. Then rewrite each sentence on the lines below.

1. Wendy and Matt took the dogs to the park, and they didn't want to go home.

   _____

   _____

2. The ball bounced off the rim and the backboard, and it broke.

   _____

   _____

3. Reggie called his friend's house, but he never answered the phone.

   _____

   _____

4. The teachers told the students they were going to visit a museum.

   _____

   _____

5. Take the top off the box, and hand it to me.

   _____

   _____

Common Core Language Grade 6 • ©2014 Newmark Learning, LLC

Name_____ Date_____

COMMON CORE
STATE STANDARD
L.6.1d

Vague Pronouns

Read each sentence and underline the vague pronoun(s). Then revise the sentence two different ways.

1. Maureen promised her mom that she would clean her room.

   a. _____

   _____

   b. _____

   _____

2. He quit his job, and it came as a big surprise to his family.

   a. _____

   _____

   b. _____

   _____

3. The teacher decided to cancel recess, and it upset the students.

   a. _____

   _____

   b. _____

   _____

4. After Mario graduated, Arnold congratulated him, and he tossed his hat into the air.

   a. _____

   _____

   b. _____

   _____

Standard English

> **COMMON CORE STATE STANDARD L.6.1e**
> Recognize variations from standard English in their own and others'
> writing and speaking, and identify and use strategies to improve
> expression in conventional language.

Explain
Grammatical problems can cause incorrect variations from standard English.

Say: *We use spoken and written language to communicate with others in a variety of settings and situations. Through dialogue, reading, and studying, we learn to use "standard English," or English that follows common structures, conventions, and vocabulary. Sometimes writers make grammatical errors, and it is important to identify and correct these errors.*

Model
Write the following paragraph on the board:

> *If you find a stray or wild animal that looks sick or injured. Call your local SPCA. Someone will tell you what to do and what not to do until help arrive. Never attempt to catch a stray or wild animal by themselves!*

Point out that the paragraph contains incorrect punctuation, a fragment, improper subject–verb agreement, and incorrect pronoun usage. The correct paragraph should look like this:

> *If you find a stray or wild animal that looks sick or injured, call your local SPCA. Someone will tell you what to do and what not to do until help arrives. Never attempt to catch a stray or wild animal by yourself!*

Guide Practice
Write the following sentences on the board. Ask a volunteer to circle the correct answer to the first sentence.

1. *Have you ever timed* (your, yours, yourself) *running speed?*
2. *Math and sports* (go, goes, going) *hand in hand.*
3. *You even need to use math to see if you have* (any, enough, much) *money to buy a hot dog!*

Ask: *Were you able to circle the correct possessive pronoun* yourself *in the first sentence?*

Repeat the procedure with the remaining sentences. Have the students circle the correct answers. Remind them to use standard English to make writing easy to read and understand.

COMMON CORE
STATE STANDARD
L.6.1e

Name_____ Date_____

Standard English

> It is important to use **standard English** and identify grammatical problems. Some of these grammatical errors include run-on sentences, sentence fragments, improper subject–verb agreement, improper verb tense, improper use of pronouns, improper use of prepositional phrases, improper use of possessives, and improper use of adjectives and adverbs.
>
> - The white space suit. (sentence fragment)
> - She goes to the bookstore yesterday. (improper verb tense)

Read the following sentences and circle the correct answer.

1. Would you like to go on a picnic (in, on, from) the park?

2. Please tell them to bring (their, theirs, they're) swimsuits and towels to the pool.

3. The odor (linger, lingering, lingered) long after we put away the chemicals we used in science class.

4. The player (kick, kicks, kicking) the ball over the goalie's head and into the net.

5. On her trip to Hollywood, she met the famous actor Brad Pitt (himself, herself)!

6. The eagles soared (highly, high) above our heads in the sky.

COMMON CORE
STATE STANDARD

L.6.1e

Name_____ Date_____

Standard English

Read the following letter. Then rewrite it, correcting the grammatical errors.

Dear City Councilman,

I am write this letter to inform he of an incident concerning my neighbor and ourselves. An old tree in my neighbors property. Hangs over my property. My neighbor does not maintain the tree, and it's limbs and leaves falls into my pristine yard.

I asked my neighbor to trim the limbs, but they refuses. I even offered to share the cost of having the tree maintained they still will not budge. Is there anything that the city can do to help you?

Sincerely,

Shirley Jones

_____

_____

_____

_____

_____

_____

_____

_____

_____

_____

Common Core Language Grade 6 • ©2014 Newmark Learning, LLC

Common Core State Standard
L.6.1e

Name_____ Date_____

Standard English

Read the following sentences and circle the correct answer.

1. Jane (blow, blown, blew) the petals off a daisy, and they fell to the ground.

2. Bertrand plodded down the stairs (clumsy, clumsily).

3. Margaret and Marjorie gave the card to (hers, their, its) great aunt.

4. I (myself, yourself) would like some time off to (relax, relaxes, relaxing).

5. She (commit, commits, committed) to the date week ago.

6. The volcano spewed hot lava (up, down, under) its sides and into the town.

7. The stars (shined, shiny) brightly in the sky above our heads.

8. The children (smile, smiles, smiling) as they listen to (its, their, theirs) teacher read aloud a story.

9. The seagull swooped down and plucked a fish (in, for, from) the ocean.

10. Our mother assured (us, we, ours) that she would be gone only a few days on her visit to (my, our, its) grandmother.

COMMON CORE
STATE STANDARD
L.6.1e

Name_____ Date_____

Standard English

Read the following sentences and rewrite them, correcting the grammatical errors.

1. Marias sister Gretchen working as an aide in a veterinary hospital.

   _____

   _____

2. After the class is over, the students returns its materials to the teacher.

   _____

   _____

3. The couple danced graceful in the music.

   _____

   _____

4. Ernesto refused to take an umbrella with her on the trip on the park.

   _____

   _____

5. The team wins the playoff game and made it to the finals.

   _____

   _____

6. The three brother walking from its house to the field to play baseball.

   _____

   _____

Common Core Language Grade 6 • ©2014 Newmark Learning, LLC

Name_____ Date_____

COMMON CORE
STATE STANDARD
L.6.1e

Standard English

Read the following passage. Then rewrite it, correcting the grammatical errors.

Photography is more than just snapping pictures of random objects or people its an art form and takes lots of practice. You need the right light, angle, and subject to capture the perfectly shot. Take your camera to you everywhere you goes, so you don't miss out on a perfect shot.

Go outdoors and exploring nature. Take advantage of the natural light that the environment offer. Capture brilliant flowers against a sunlit sky. Don't be afraid. Of a little rain or cloudy skies. Gray or white clouds provides the perfect background for snapping shots of birds and squirrels.

_____

_____

_____

_____

_____

_____

_____

_____

_____

_____

_____

_____

_____

_____

_____

_____

_____

COMMON CORE
STATE STANDARD

L.6.2a

Use Punctuation (Commas, Parentheses, and Dashes) to Set Off Elements

COMMON CORE STATE STANDARD L.6.2a
Use punctuation (commas, parentheses, dashes) to set off
nonrestrictive/parenthetical elements.

Explain
Writers use commas, dashes, and parentheses to set off nonrestrictive/
parenthetical elements in writing.

Say: *Writers often add details to a basic sentence. If they simply provide extra
information and the sentence would still make sense without it, the sentence
is considered nonrestrictive or parenthetical. Commas are the most common
way to set off nonrestrictive elements at the beginning, middle, or end of a
sentence. Parentheses are used to set off remarks, tips, or facts. Dashes are
used to give a nonrestrictive element more emphasis or to set apart items in a
series that are already punctuated with commas.*

Model
Write the following sentences on the board:

1. *My mother, who has a degree in physics, works as a teacher at my
   school.*
2. *Most maps contain symbols—numbers, letters, lines, dots, and colors that
   represent something else.*
3. *Capua, Italy, is a town 130 miles (209 kilometers) south of Rome.*

Point out that the first sentence uses commas around the nonrestrictive
element. Point out that the second sentence uses a dash to set apart items in a
series. The third sentence uses parentheses to add a measurement.

Guide Practice
Write the following sentences on the board. Ask a volunteer to add commas,
dashes, or parentheses to the first sentence.

1. *My dog a toy fox terrier likes to bark at everything he sees.*
2. *My sister who is four years older than I am works at a boutique.*
3. *They noticed one thing missing from the table the food.*

Repeat the procedure with the remaining sentences. Have the students
determine which type of punctuation belongs in each sentence. Remind them
that a nonrestrictive element can be an explanation, description, definition,
example, comment, or other type of information the author chooses to support
a text.

Name_____ Date_____

COMMON CORE
STATE STANDARD
L.6.2a

Use Commas to Set Off Elements

Nonrestrictive elements are not necessary to make the meaning of a sentence clear and contain additional information. **Commas** are the most common way to set off nonrestrictive elements at the beginning, middle, or end of a sentence.

- The principal dancer, who went to my high school, is graceful.
- The book report, which I have yet to write, is due next week.

Read each sentence. Then add commas to set off the nonrestrictive elements.

1. My brother whom I miss terribly is away at college.

2. The fortieth president of the United States Ronald Reagan was also an actor.

3. The locksmith used a slim-jim a thin strip of metal used to open locks to pry open the car door.

4. Janie went to see a podiatrist a foot doctor because she felt pain in her heel.

5. Matt who was late for school again rushed to get dressed and darted out the door.

6. Mr. Bowie who is a member of the British Historical Society will be the speaker at our next meeting.

COMMON CORE
STATE STANDARD
L.6.2a

Name_____ Date_____

Use Commas to Set Off Elements

Rewrite each sentence. Add a nonrestrictive element to each sentence, using commas appropriately.

1. Uncle Todd's truck needs new tires.

_____

_____

2. The waiters set up the tables and chairs.

_____

_____

3. Jane Austen wrote the book *Pride and Prejudice.*

_____

_____

4. Sal's Pizzeria serves pizza and hoagies.

_____

_____

5. George Washington was the first president of the United States.

_____

_____

Name_____ Date_____

Common Core
State Standard
L.6.2a

Use Parentheses to Set Off Elements

> **Parentheses** can be used to set off remarks, tips, or facts within a sentence. Parentheses are normally used to set off the least important information in a sentence. Authors also use parentheses to speak directly to readers.
>
> - ". . . story-telling (whether the stories are true or made up) is a thing you're taught, just as English boys and girls are taught essay-writing." —C.S. Lewis, *The Horse and His Boy*
> - We saw a small, red bird (a cardinal?) in the tree yesterday.

Read each sentence. Then add parentheses to set off nonrestrictive elements.

1. J. K. Rowling's *Harry Potter and the Sorcerer's Stone* 1997 was the first book in the Harry Potter series.

2. Astronauts Neil Armstrong and Buzz Aldrin were part of the first mission July 20, 1969 to the moon.

3. Martin Luther King Jr. is best known for a speech "I Have a Dream" that he gave during the March on Washington for Jobs and Freedom in 1963.

4. In 1920 women were granted the right to vote with the addition of an amendment Nineteenth Amendment to the Constitution.

5. My mom cooked us spaghetti and meatballs my favorite for dinner.

COMMON CORE
STATE STANDARD
L.6.2a

Name_____ Date_____

Use Parentheses to Set Off Elements

Rewrite each sentence. Add a nonrestrictive element to each sentence and use parentheses to set off the elements.

1. My neighbor's dog can jump almost as high as the fence in the yard.

_____

_____

2. Mark Twain wrote *The Adventures of Tom Sawyer.*

_____

_____

3. Nina is not allowed to have a pet because she has allergies.

_____

_____

4. Tickets for the event will be available until the day of the event.

_____

_____

5. *The Wizard of Oz* is the story of a girl named Dorothy who gets lost in the land of Oz with her dog, Toto.

_____

_____

Name_____ Date_____

Common Core State Standard

L.6.2a

Use Dashes to Set Off Elements

Dashes can be used to give a nonrestrictive element more emphasis. Dashes are used more informally in writing, and are used to emphasize and set off important information.

- All four countries—England, Greece, Spain, and Italy—are beautiful.
- Even the simplest tasks—washing my hair, brushing my teeth—were hard to do after I broke my leg.

Read each sentence. Add dashes to set off nonrestrictive elements.

1. Her choices in different cuisines from Thai to Indian show her willingness to try new things.

2. The brothers Guillermo, Marco, Roberto, and Julio all played on the football team during high school.

3. Her mother a Girl Scout leader, a coach, and a full-time dentist does not have enough time to participate in the annual bake sale.

4. Margaret Thatcher was the first woman and the longest-serving prime minister of the United Kingdom.

5. Heirloom roses grow in many different colors red, pink, peach, orange, and yellow.

COMMON CORE
STATE STANDARD

L.6.2a

Name_____ Date_____

Use Dashes to Set Off Elements

Rewrite each sentence. Add a nonrestrictive element to each sentence and use dashes to set off the elements.

1. His decision to leave the company was based on one reason.

_____

_____

2. They learned about different marine animals in biology class.

_____

_____

3. Amy read the list from the cookbook and added the ingredients to the bowl.

_____

_____

4. My grandfather enjoys reading the phone book for fun.

_____

_____

5. She demanded one thing from her students.

_____

_____

Name_____ Date_____

COMMON CORE
STATE STANDARD
L.6.2a

Use Punctuation (Commas, Parentheses, and Dashes) to Set Off Elements

Write two sentences using commas to set off nonrestrictive elements.

1. _____

    _____

2. _____

    _____

Write two sentences using parentheses to set off nonrestrictive elements.

3. _____

    _____

4. _____

    _____

Write two sentences using dashes to set off nonrestrictive elements.

5. _____

    _____

6. _____

    _____

COMMON CORE
STATE STANDARD
L.6.2b

Spell Correctly

> **COMMON CORE STATE STANDARD L.6.2b**
> Spell correctly.

Explain
Different types of reference materials can help writers spell words correctly.

Say: *Sometimes writers must consult reference materials to ensure they spell words correctly. In addition to using print and online dictionaries and a spell-checker on a computer, writers can sometimes consult glossaries in the back of textbooks for spellings of words. Classroom word banks or classroom spelling rules anchor charts are other tools to use to determine the correct spellings of words.*

Model
Write the following words on the board:

  personal   *personnel*

Explain that *personal* is an adjective meaning "belonging or relating to a particular person." *Personnel* is a noun meaning "people who work for a particular company or organization." Point out that using the correct spelling of words is important because misspelling a word can change its meaning and the meaning of writing.

Guide Practice
Write the following misspelled words on the board. Ask a volunteer to look up the correct spelling of the first word.

  photografer   *enthoosism*   *proffesional*   *qantity*

Ask: *Were you able to determine the correct spelling for* photographer?

Repeat the procedure with the remaining words. Have the students practice looking up the correct spellings of words. Remind them that sometimes it helps to guess at the spelling of a word before trying to find it in a dictionary, a glossary, or other reference material.

Name_____ Date_____

COMMON CORE
STATE STANDARD
L.6.2b

Spell Correctly

Print or online dictionaries, classroom spelling rules anchor charts, and a computer spell-checker help us find the proper way to **spell** a word. Properly spelled words make writing clear and easy to understand.

- She drew a <u>strait</u> line on the paper. (incorrect)
- She drew a <u>straight</u> line on the paper. (correct)

Read each pair of words. Then circle the one spelled correctly. Reference materials, such as a dictionary, may be used.

1. accidentally   accidentaly
2. guarantee   garauntee
3. fasinate   fascinate
4. attendence   attendance
5. forein   foreign
6. occassion   occasion
7. judgment   judgement
8. necessary   neccessary
9. privilege   privlege
10. separate   seperate

11. vacuum   vaccum
12. noticeable   noticable
13. immediatly   immediately
14. desperatly   desperately
15. embarrass   embarass
16. mischievus   mischievous
17. physical   pysical
18. beleive   believe
19. psychic   phsycic
20. arguement   argument

COMMON CORE
STATE STANDARD
L.6.2b

Name_____ Date_____

Spell Correctly

Circle the misspelled word in each sentence and rewrite it correctly on the line.

1. The athlete was rewarded for his hard work when he won the tornament.

   _____

2. Ruby needed help and asked for assisstence with the project.

   _____

3. The character in the film cried, "I thought I could trust her, but she decieved me!"

   _____

4. Dad was not able to repair the leaky faucet, so he hired a proffessional plumber.

   _____

5. During the lesson, the teacher illistarted the differences between algebra and geometry.

   _____

6. Using the correct formula is essential to solving the problem.

   _____

7. The map showed numerus routes to take to get to our destination.

   _____

8. I axidentally knocked the figurine off the table, and it smashed on the floor.

   _____

Common Core Language Grade 6 • ©2014 Newmark Learning, LLC

Name_____ Date_____

Common Core
State Standard
L.6.2b

Spell Correctly

**Circle the word or words that correctly complete each sentence.
If necessary, use spelling reference materials to find the correct
answers.**

1. Her older sister's blouse was too (loose/lose) on her.

2. They (accepted/excepted) the dinner invitation from their friends.

3. Frank thanked his coach for the good (advise/advice) he gave him
   on improving his game.

4. The zookeeper could not explain the (bazaar/bizarre) behavior of
   the elephants.

5. The race (course/coarse) included hills, rough terrain, and obstacles.

6. Before she handed in her book report, Teresa double-checked it to
   (insure/ensure) she had no errors.

7. The man (peddled/pedaled) his goods to the people who passed by
   his table at the flea market.

8. The truck idled (stationary/stationery) while the employee unloaded
   the packages.

9. The (principle/principal) decided to close the school because the
   heating unit was not working properly.

10. Jose grabbed the pitcher and (poured/pored) the juice into a glass
    for his guest.

COMMON CORE
STATE STANDARD

L.6.3a

Vary Sentences for Meaning, Interest, and Style

> **COMMON CORE STATE STANDARD L.6.3a**
> Vary sentence patterns for meaning, reader/listener interest, and style.

Explain
Expanding, combining, and reducing sentences are ways to improve writing.

Say: *There are three main types of sentences: simple, compound, and complex. Sometimes sentences fail to give enough information, provide choppy information, or give too much information. By expanding, combining, and reducing sentences, writers create sentences that are meaningful, will keep readers' interest, and project a style that is easy to read, follow, and understand.*

Model
Write the following sentences on the board:

1. *She may go.*
2. *Michaela may go on a trip. She may spend time with her grandmother.*
3. *Michaela may go on a trip but she does not know if she could. Her parents must first give her permission or not and if they let her go she will be able to spend time with her grandmother.*

Point out that the first sentence lacks information. The second sentence provides choppy information. The third sentence contains too much information and is hard to follow. Explain that these sentences can be fixed by expanding, combining, and reducing.

Guide Practice
Write the following sentences on the board. Ask a volunteer to expand the first sentence.

1. *Harold ran.* (Harold ran in a 5k race.)
2. *Harold trains to run in races. He trains six days a week. He competed in a 5k race.* (Harold trained six days a week to compete in a 5k race.
3. *Harold enjoys running in races and he has been training to run in another 5k race for six or maybe seven months now because he ran in his first 5k race in February.* (Harold, who enjoys running, competed in a 5k race in February. He has trained the last seven months to compete in another 5k race.)

Have the students combine the choppy sentences in the second example and reduce the sentences in the third example. Remind them that expanding, combining, and reducing sentences will make their writing meaningful, keep readers' interest, and project a style that is easy to read, follow, and understand.

Name_____ Date_____

COMMON CORE
STATE STANDARD
L.6.3a

Vary Sentences for Meaning

It is important to construct clear sentences when speaking and writing. If incorrect verb tenses or unclear pronouns are used, for example, sentence **meaning** can be unclear to readers. By **varying sentence structure** (arranging clauses, different subjects, creative verbs, adding details, among others), the meaning of sentences can change.

- After the teacher gave Susan the paper, <u>she</u> walked away angrily. (Who is *she*—the teacher or Susan?)
- After the teacher gave Susan the paper, <u>Susan</u> walked away angrily.

Each sentence below contains a grammatical error, causing the sentence meaning to be unclear. Rewrite each sentence on the lines, correcting the error.

1. The man went to the store because you needed bread.

_____

_____

2. Michael went to the doctor, and he said he was sick.

_____

_____

3. Derek smiled at his father as he threw him the baseball.

_____

_____

4. Liz and Megan are sisters, but she has always been taller.

_____

_____

COMMON CORE
STATE STANDARD
L.6.3a

Name_____ Date_____

Vary Sentences for Meaning

Rewrite each sentence below two different ways, changing the meaning of the sentence.

1. The greatest thing was when I caught the fly ball.

a. _____

_____

b. _____

_____

2. It would be amazing to go into space.

a. _____

_____

b. _____

_____

3. When she sang my favorite song, I was so excited!

a. _____

_____

b. _____

_____

Name_____ Date_____

COMMON CORE
STATE STANDARD
L.6.3a

Vary Sentences for Interest

Varying the structure of sentences when speaking or writing is important in order to sustain the **interest** of the listener or reader. In addition, adding details to sentences can increase interest.

- A package arrived.
- A package arrived for me on Tuesday.
- A mysterious package arrived on my doorstep Tuesday afternoon.
- A mysterious package covered in newspaper arrived on my doorstep Tuesday afternoon, and I was curious as to what it contained.

Rewrite each sentence below, adding details for interest.

1. The knight put away his sword.

   _____

   _____

   _____

2. The castle fortress is strong.

   _____

   _____

   _____

3. The black flag billowed in the wind.

   _____

   _____

   _____

4. The two dragons are best friends.

   _____

   _____

   _____

COMMON CORE
STATE STANDARD
L.6.3a

Name_____ Date_____

Vary Sentences for Interest

Rewrite the following paragraphs, adding details to make them more interesting.

1. We went to an amusement park. It was fun. We rode many different rides. The food was good. It was a good day.

    _____

    _____

    _____

    _____

    _____

    _____

    _____

    _____

2. I went to a museum with my class. We spent all day there. There were many paintings. My favorite painting was there.

    _____

    _____

    _____

    _____

    _____

    _____

    _____

    _____

Name_____ Date_____

COMMON CORE
STATE STANDARD
L.6.3a

Vary Sentences for Style

Style reflects a writer's voice, and writers must maintain a consistent style when writing. Each type of writing requires a different style. For example, would you use the same style for a newspaper article as you would for a short story? It's important to **vary** the style by using a combination of simple, complex, and compound sentences. Below are rules for academic style writing:

- The style should be formal. It should not contain slang or abbreviations.
- It should be written from the third person point of view.
- It should be focused on the facts, not the writer's opinion.
- The tone should be neutral.

On the lines below, rewrite the paragraph so that its tone and style are consistently formal.

1. In New Mexico there's this National Monument called White Sands. There is a lot of white sand dunes there and the sand is rare and called gypsum sand. It's like 275 square miles. Tons of animals and plants live there even though it's super hard for them to survive because the weather is bad there's little water.

_____

_____

_____

_____

_____

_____

_____

_____

_____

_____

_____

COMMON CORE
STATE STANDARD

L.6.3a

Name_____ Date_____

Vary Sentences for Style

Rewrite the following sentence according to each style below.

I was anxious about Friday.

1. complex sentence

_____

_____

_____

2. compound sentence

_____

_____

_____

3. an interrogative sentence

_____

_____

_____

4. a sentence in present tense

_____

_____

_____

5. a sentence with two subjects and two verbs

_____

_____

_____

Name_____ Date_____

COMMON CORE
STATE STANDARD
L.6.3a

Vary Sentences for Meaning, Interest, and Style

Imagine your class is taking a trip to the moon, and you are covering the story for your school newspaper. Write an article featuring details of the trip, including what you will be doing, what you are bringing, and why you are going. Remember to vary sentences for style, meaning, and interest.

_____

_____

_____

_____

_____

_____

_____

_____

_____

_____

_____

_____

_____

_____

_____

_____

_____

_____

COMMON CORE
STATE STANDARD
L.6.3b

Maintain Consistency in Style and Tone

> **COMMON CORE STATE STANDARD L.6.3b**
> Maintain consistency in style and tone.

Explain
Different types of writing require differences in style and tone, but a single, appropriate style and tone must be maintained within each document.

Say: *Style in writing is a technical term for how a writer purposely creates certain effects using language and writing mechanics. The purpose of the text, whether it is a legal contract or a letter to a friend, determines the style. The emotion or attitude of the writer is expressed through tone. Sometimes written material can be correct but still be hard to understand. Sometimes a word or sentence doesn't quite fit, or a statement isn't appropriate for the type of document in which it appears. The presence of an idiomatic expression in a business document or a six-syllable word in an informal narrative can throw off the reader. Problems such as these are related to style and tone.*

Model
Write the following sentences on the board:

1. *Hey, Johnny, will you meet me at Columbus Park on Saturday morning?*
2. *Mr. and Mrs. Raymon Blanco request the honor of your presence at the marriage of their daughter Anita Rose to Mr. Juan Roberto Rivera on Saturday, September 27 at Columbus Park.*

Point out that the basic messages are similar—someone wants someone else to go to a certain park at a certain time. But the purpose of each requires a completely different style and tone.

Guide Practice
Write the following phrases and words on the board. Ask a volunteer to identify the tone of the first phrase.

feeling poorly, ill, diagnosis, unwell, under the weather, pathology

Ask: *Were you able to identify the tone of the expression* feeling poorly? Repeat the procedure with the rest of the words and phrases.

Have the students write the types of documents that each word or phrase could be used in. Remind them that some words can be neutral enough to fit into many types of writing.

Name_____ Date_____

COMMON CORE
STATE STANDARD
L.6.3b

Maintain Consistency in Style

When writing or speaking, it is important to be consistent in **style**. Style refers to the way writing is put together, including choices the writer makes about specific sentence patterns and words. Style also differs based on the audience. Below are common tips to help you **maintain consistent style**:

- Avoid using too many words, especially "filler" words that do not add meaning.
- Choose words that have precise meaning.
- Vary sentence length and structure.

Rewrite each sentence for the audience listed. Remember to maintain consistent and appropriate style.

1. **Newspaper**

   One of these days maybe somebody will find a cure for zits.

   _____

   _____

2. **E-mail to a close friend**

   In all likelihood we will attend the cinema in the near future.

   _____

   _____

3. **Graded paper for a teacher**

   Well, for one thing, Clara Barton did things with the Office of Missing Soldiers after the Civil War was pretty much over.

   _____

   _____

4. **Letter to a state senator**

   I seriously can't stand the way the highways are so full of potholes that it rattles your teeth just to go to work.

   _____

   _____

COMMON CORE
STATE STANDARD

L.6.3b

Name_____ Date_____

Maintain Consistency in Style

Write a paragraph about your favorite sport, activity, or hobby. Imagine you are writing the paragraph for someone who has never heard of your subject. Carefully choose your style, and maintain it throughout the paragraph.

_____

_____

_____

_____

_____

_____

_____

_____

_____

_____

_____

_____

_____

_____

_____

_____

_____

COMMON CORE
STATE STANDARD
L.6.3b

Name_____ Date_____

Maintain Consistency in Tone

Tone refers to how something is said or written. It conveys the writer's attitude toward the audience and subject matter. Word choice is very important when conveying a certain tone. This chart illustrates different tones used in formal and informal writing.

Informal	Formal
light, humorous	serious
personal, casual	objective, impersonal
experimental	reasonable, reserved
simple, blunt	elaborate

Read each word. Then write a sentence that includes the word and gives a context for the tone of the word.

1. bitter _____

_____

2. gloomy _____

_____

3. fanciful _____

_____

4. whimsical _____

_____

5. malicious _____

_____

6. artificial _____

_____

COMMON CORE
STATE STANDARD
L.6.3b

Name_____ Date_____

Maintain Consistency in Tone

Read the paragraph below. Then, rewrite the paragraph as if it were part of an academic paper. Remember to use the appropriate tone.

Leonardo da Vinci was like, one of the most famous Renaissance Men to ever live. He painted, did art, was a scupltor, scientist, and an inventor. People think his favorite inventions were his flying machines, which were super cool. He loved the idea that people could fly one day! Watching animals fly totally influenced his ideas about flying, especially bats. And while da Vinci's flying machine probably would've flown once it was actually in the air, he could not figure out how to get it off the ground. Still, da Vinci was really cool and influenced a lot of scientists today.

_____

_____

_____

_____

_____

_____

_____

_____

_____

_____

_____

Lesson Plan Teacher Worksheet
Vocabulary Acquisition and Use

The lessons in this section are organized in the same order as the Common Core Language Standards for vocabulary acquisition and use. Each mini-lesson provides specific, explicit instruction for a Language standard and is followed by multiple practice pages. Use the following chart to track the standards students have practiced. You may wish to revisit mini-lessons and practice pages a second time for spiral review.

Common Core State Standard	Mini-Lessons and Practice	Page	Complete (✓)	Review (✓)
L.6.4a	Mini-Lesson 10: Use Context Clues	58		
	Practice: Use Context Clues—Overall Meaning	59		
	Practice: Use Context Clues—Position and Function	61		
L.6.4b	Mini-Lesson 11: Greek and Latin Affixes and Roots	64		
	Practice: Greek and Latin Affixes—Prefixes	65		
	Practice: Greek and Latin Affixes—Suffixes	66		
	Practice: Greek and Latin Roots	69		
L.6.4c	Mini-Lesson 12: Consult Reference Materials for Pronunciation and Meaning	76		
	Practice: Consult Reference Materials for Pronunciation	77		
	Practice: Consult Reference Materials for Meaning	79		
L.6.4d	Mini-Lesson 13: Verify Meanings of Words	82		
	Practice: Verify Meanings of Words	83		
L.6.5a	Mini-Lesson 14: Interpret Figures of Speech	86		
	Practice: Interpret Figures of Speech	87		
L.6.5b	Mini-Lesson 15: Word Relationships	90		
	Practice: Word Relationships—Cause/Effect	91		
	Practice: Word Relationships—Part/Whole	93		
	Practice: Word Relationships—Item/Category	95		
L.6.5c	Mini-Lesson 16: Distinguish Connotations	98		
	Practice: Distinguish Connotations	99		

COMMON CORE
STATE STANDARD

L.6.4a

Use Context Clues

> **COMMON CORE STATE STANDARD L.6.4a**
> Use context (e.g., the overall meaning of a sentence or paragraph; a word's position or function in a sentence) as a clue to the meaning of a word or phrase.

Explain

Use context clues to determine the meaning of unfamiliar words or phrases.

Say: *As readers, we sometimes need to figure out the meaning of new words or phrases. We can use context clues in sentences and paragraphs to help us determine the meanings of words. We can also use an unfamiliar word's position or function in a sentence to determine its meaning. Using the overall meaning of a sentence or paragraph as well as the word's position and function in a sentence help you picture and understand what new words or phrases mean.*

Model

Write the following sentences on the board:

1. *Because he signed his name to the contract, he is liable for any damages.*
2. *The office supply store has a great line of binders.*

Point out that the overall meaning of the first sentence helps you determine the meaning of *liable* is "responsible." Point out that in the second sentence, you need to rely on the position and function of the word *line* to determine its meaning. The word *line* follows the adjective *great*, so we can assume that it's a noun. From the meaning of the sentence, we can figure out that *line* means "a type of merchandise the store carries."

Guide Practice

Write the following sentences on the board. Ask a volunteer to determine the meaning of the underlined word in the first sentence.

1. *The water <u>quenched</u> his thirst on the hot day.*
2. *The mom sang a <u>lullaby</u> to help her newborn fall asleep.*

Ask: *Were you able to determine that* quenched *means "stopped the thirst"?*

Repeat the procedure with the remaining sentence. Have the students determine the meaning of the underlined word in the sentence. Remind them to use the context of the sentence and the position and function of the unfamiliar word to determine its meaning.

Name_____ Date_____

COMMON CORE
STATE STANDARD
L.6.4a

Use Context Clues—Overall Meaning

Use **context clues** in sentences and paragraphs to determine the meanings of unfamiliar words. The **overall meaning** of a sentence or paragraph helps you understand what new words mean.

- If you <u>procrastinate</u> any longer, you will not finish your homework before it is due. (*procrastinate*: to delay, postpone)
- The police had to <u>apprehend</u> the suspect before he escaped. (*apprehend*: to arrest, catch)

Read each sentence. Then use context clues to help you fill in the blanks with the correct word from the box below.

shy	bent	story	conversation	guess

1. Because the last page of the book was missing, I could only <u>speculate</u> what happened.

   _____

2. The <u>dialogue</u> between the characters in the movie made us laugh.

   _____

3. The wooden picnic table <u>warped</u> after it was left outside in the harsh winter weather.

   _____

4. The <u>bashful</u> little girl hid behind her mother when they entered the building.

   _____

5. The teacher told us an amusing <u>anecdote</u> about his son.

   _____

COMMON CORE
STATE STANDARD
L.6.4a

Name_____ Date_____

Use Context Clues—Overall Meaning

Read the passage below. Then use context clues to help you fill in the blanks with the correct word or phrase from the box below.

propose	absolute	compose	reject
formidable	maintained	introduced	sponsored

The president of the United States is the chief of the government,

but he does not have _____ power. He plays

a _____ role in the lawmaking process.

First, a representative drafts a bill. Then, the bill becomes

_____, or supported. The bill is then ready to

be _____ to the House of Representatives.

Once Congress, which is made up of the Senate and the House of

Representatives, approves a bill, they send it to the president. The

president must then approve or _____ the

bill. If he approves the bill, it becomes a law. The president cannot

_____, or write, a bill to become a law. He

can _____ ideas to Congress, who can then

decide whether to use the president's ideas to write a bill. After the

bill becomes a law, the Supreme Court decides whether or not a

bill is constitutional. This is how a system of checks and balances is

_____ in the United States government.

Common Core Language Grade 6 • ©2014 Newmark Learning, LLC

Name_____ Date_____

COMMON CORE
STATE STANDARD
L.6.4a

Use Context Clues—Position and Function

Another way to use **context clues** to figure out the meaning of a word is by looking at a word's **position** or **function** in a sentence. For example, if a word you don't know is where a verb would be in a sentence, that unknown word is probably a verb.

- The <u>frigid</u> water made her teeth chatter. (*Water* is the noun, so *frigid* must be an adjective meaning "very cold.")
- I <u>fractured</u> my arm and had to wear a cast. (*I* is the subject, *arm* is the object, so *fractured* must be a verb meaning "to break.")

Read each sentence. Using context clues, circle the correct meaning of the underlined word in each sentence.

1. Neville came up with a <u>novel</u> approach to completing the exercises.
   a. new and different
   b. a fictional story

2. Dad could not find an <u>outlet</u> to plug in the new appliance.
   a. a place or opening through which something is let out
   b. a receptacle for the plug of an electrical device

3. My grandmother is an excellent <u>sewer</u> and makes her own clothes.
   a. one who sews
   b. a pipe that carries wastewater and refuse

4. Brent placed a deck of cards under the leg of the kitchen table to make it <u>stable</u>.
   a. a shelter for animals
   b. steady

5. Mom browsed through the <u>produce</u> section of the grocery store in search of apples for pie.
   a. fresh fruits and vegetables
   b. to make something

COMMON CORE
STATE STANDARD
L.6.4a

Name_____ Date_____

Use Context Clues—Position and Function

Read each sentence. Using context clues, circle the correct meaning of the underlined word in each sentence.

1. The soccer coach asked Matthew to <u>track</u> his teammates' goals.
   a. a mark left by a person or animal
   b. to follow or keep count of something

2. The new clues in the case <u>clouded</u> the detective's mind.
   a. to make unclear or confuse
   b. to cover the sky with white or gray masses

3. Before they could go fishing, they first needed a <u>permit</u>.
   a. a license or warrant allowing permission to do something
   b. to allow or give permission

4. Due to the dry weather, the crop's <u>yield</u> was not as plentiful as it was the previous year.
   a. amount of something produced
   b. to stop or halt

5. The farmer attached the <u>harness</u> to the horse and then to the wagon.
   a. to use or control
   b. a set of straps placed on an animal to pull something heavy

6. The toddler cried and <u>stamped</u> his foot when he didn't get his way.
   a. to bring the foot down heavily to the ground
   b. to mark something with a device or tool

Common Core Language Grade 6 • ©2014 Newmark Learning, LLC

Name_____ Date_____

COMMON CORE
STATE STANDARD
L.6.4a

Use Context Clues—Overall Meaning and Position and Function

Read each sentence. Then choose a word from the box below that matches the underlined word in each sentence.

brilliant	**products**	**brisk**	**bombarded**

1. Bethany browsed the aisles of the store looking at the <u>merchandise</u> on the shelves. _____

2. The geometry teacher <u>inundated</u> the class with information about the many different types of triangles. _____

3. The <u>radiant</u> sun reflected off the clear lake. _____

4. Daily <u>vigorous</u> exercise is healthy for the body. _____

Read each sentence and use the context clues to determine the correct meaning of the underlined word in the sentence.

5. She <u>flushed</u> her eyes with water to remove the dust particles.
   a. turned red
   b. rinsed

6. Dad yelled at the children to get <u>down</u> from the tall tree.
   a. to go from a high to low place or position
   b. to eat something quickly

7. Mrs. Kildarie will <u>address</u> the noisy class in a stern yet calm manner.
   a. a place where someone lives
   b. speak to

COMMON CORE
STATE STANDARD
L.6.4b

Greek and Latin Affixes and Roots

> **COMMON CORE STATE STANDARD L.6.4b**
> Use common, grade-appropriate Greek or Latin affixes and roots as clues to the meaning of a word (e.g., *audience, auditory, audible*).

Explain

The Greek and Latin languages contributed many words and word parts to English. Learning about Greek and Latin affixes and roots can help readers and writers understand and use more words.

Say: *Many words in the English language are based on Greek and Latin roots. Many of our most common and useful prefixes and suffixes come from the Greek and Latin languages as well. Learning these word parts helps readers figure out the meanings of new words and helps writers select and spell appropriate words as well.*

Model

Write the following words on the board.

audience   auditorium   audible

Point out that these words have something in common. They all contain the root *aud*. Ask students to think about what *aud* means. Figuring this out can help to determine the meanings of all of these words. Explain that *aud* is a Latin root meaning "hear." Each word also has other parts that add other meanings. (For example, *-orium* means "place for.") An *audience* is a group of people who hear. An *auditorium* is a place for hearing. *Audible* means "able to be heard." Knowing about Greek and Latin roots and affixes helps us find these meanings.

Guide Practice

Write the following root and meaning on the board. Ask a volunteer to list other words that contain the root.

graph—Greek root meaning "write"

Ask: *Were you able to come up with some words containing the root* graph? Ask the students to tell how these words are related.

Have students come up with meanings of the other word parts of these words. Remind them that word parts help us figure out the meaning of new words.

Name_____ Date_____

Common Core
State Standard
L.6.4b

Greek and Latin Affixes—Prefixes

An **affix** is added to the beginning (prefix) or end (suffix) of a root word. **Greek and Latin prefixes** can tell us what words mean. Each prefix has a different definition, which gives clues as to the meaning of unknown words.

Prefix	Meaning	Example
fin-	end	final
post-	after	postscript (p.s.)

Read the definition of the provided prefixes below. Think of a word containing each prefix, and write it on the line. Then use each word in a sentence.

1. Prefix: **de-**　　　　　Definition: away, off, remove

   Example word: _____

   Example sentence: _____

   _____

2. Prefix: **non-**　　　　Definition: not, not any

   Example word: _____

   Example sentence: _____

   _____

3. Prefix: **pre-**　　　　Definition: before, earlier than

   Example word: _____

   Example sentence: _____

   _____

4. Prefix: **sub-**　　　　Definition: under, below

   Example word: _____

   Example sentence: _____

   _____

COMMON CORE
STATE STANDARD
L.6.4b

Name_____ Date_____

Greek and Latin Affixes—Suffixes

An **affix** is added to the beginning (prefix) or end (suffix) of a root word. **Greek and Latin suffixes** can tell us what words mean. Each suffix has a different definition, which gives clues as to the meaning of unknown words or changes the word's part of speech.

Suffix	Meaning	Example
-dom	quality, realm	king<u>dom</u>
-ine	nature of	medic<u>ine</u>

Read the definition of the provided suffixes below. Think of a word containing each suffix, and write it on the line. Then use each word in a sentence.

1. Suffix: **-able** or **-ible**   Definition: capable of, worthy of

   Example word: _____

   Example sentence: _____

   _____

2. Suffix: **-ment**   Definition: act of, state of

   Example word: _____

   Example sentence: _____

   _____

3. Suffix: **-ify**   Definition: to cause, to make

   Example word: _____

   Example sentence: _____

   _____

4. Suffix: **-ous**   Definition: full of, having

   Example word: _____

   Example sentence: _____

   _____

Name_____ Date_____

COMMON CORE
STATE STANDARD
L.6.4b

Greek and Latin Affixes

For each word, identify the Greek or Latin affix. Then write the meaning of the affix and the word.

1. Word: **interweave**

   Affix: _____

   Affix definition: _____

   Word definition: _____

2. Word: **nonstop**

   Affix: _____

   Affix definition: _____

   Word definition: _____

3. Word: **purify**

   Affix: _____

   Affix definition: _____

   Word definition: _____

4. Word: **marvelous**

   Affix: _____

   Affix definition: _____

   Word definition: _____

5. Word: **preexist**

   Affix: _____

   Affix definition: _____

   Word definition: _____

6. Word: **transatlantic**

   Affix: _____

   Affix definition: _____

   Word definition: _____

Common Core
State Standard
L.6.4b

Name_____ Date_____

Greek and Latin Affixes

Read the chart below. Using the provided information, fill in the missing boxes.

Greek & Latin Affix	Meaning	English Word	Definition
1.	"apart; away from"	absent	
2.		antibacterial	active against bacteria
3.		biweekly	taking place every two weeks, or twice in one week
4.	"out"	exterior	
5.	"between"	interact	
6.		visible	able to be seen
7.	"native of"	Canadian	
8.		actress	a female actor
9.	"nature of; like"	artistic	
10.	"make"	simplify	

Name_____ Date_____

Greek and Latin Roots

> Most words have **Greek and Latin roots**, which help to provide clues to the meanings of words. Understanding the roots of unknown words allows us to figure out the definitions of difficult words. Some words can have two root words.
>
> <u>tele</u> (far)   +   <u>scope</u> (look at)   =   telescope
> <u>auto</u> (self) +   <u>graph</u> (write)   =   autograph

Read each root and sample words based on that root. Using this information, circle the correct definition of each root.

1. Root: **photo**

   Sample words: *photograph*, *photosynthesis*

   Root definition:

   A. change   **B.** small   **C.** light   **D.** move

2. Root: **scop**

   Sample words: *telescope, microscope*

   Root definition:

   A. mix   **B.** see   **C.** new   **D.** full

3. Root: **loc**

   Sample words: *location, dislocate*

   Root definition:

   A. place   **B.** time   **C.** few   **D.** fix

4. Root: **soci**

   Sample words: *social, associate*

   Root definition:

   A. cover   **B.** climb   **C.** wish   **D.** group

COMMON CORE
STATE STANDARD
L.6.4b

Name_____ Date_____

Greek and Latin Roots

Read the Greek or Latin root and its definition, and then each sentence. Then write the word that best fits the sentence on the line. Use a dictionary for assistance.

1. <u>Root</u>: **act** ("do")

   "Please try to _____ (enact, react, transact) with surprise when Aunt Millie gives you the same birthday gift you get every year," said Mom.

2. <u>Root</u>: **meter** ("measure")

   Meteorologists use tools called _____ (barometers, micrometers, thermometers) to measure the pressure in our atmosphere.

3. <u>Root</u>: **aqua** ("water")

   My aunt stocked her _____ (aquarium, aquamarine, aquatic) with a collection of vividly colored fish from around the world.

4. <u>Root</u>: **port** ("carry")

   Dad hired a moving van to _____ (import, transport, comport) our belongings to our new apartment.

5. <u>Root</u>: **volv** ("turn")

   I hope my sister doesn't _____ (revolve, evolve, involve) me in her ridiculous plan.

Name_____ Date_____

COMMON CORE
STATE STANDARD
L.6.4b

Greek and Latin Roots

Complete the chart below by writing an English word that contains each Greek or Latin root. Then write a sentence using each word. Include context clues that explain the word's meaning.

Root	Meaning	Word
bio	"life"	
graph	"write, written"	
vac	"empty"	
civ	"citizen, person"	

1. _____

   _____

   _____

2. _____

   _____

   _____

3. _____

   _____

   _____

4. _____

   _____

   _____

COMMON CORE
STATE STANDARD
L.6.4b

Name_____ Date_____

Greek and Latin Roots

For each of the Greek or Latin roots below, find two modern words based on this root. Then, write a sentence correctly using each word. Include context clues that explain the word's meaning.

1. Root: **form**
   Meaning: "form," "simple"

Modern Word Based on Root	Sentence Using this Word

2. Root: **cycle**
   Meaning: "circle"

Modern Word Based on Root	Sentence Using this Word

3. Root: **port**
   Meaning: "carry"

Modern Word Based on Root	Sentence Using this Word

Name_____ Date_____

COMMON CORE
STATE STANDARD
L.6.4b

Greek and Latin Roots and Affixes

Use the chart below to discover the meaning of each word. Then, write a sentence with each word. Include context clues that explain the word's meaning.

Root/Affix	Definition	Root/Affix	Definition
ed	*eat*	exo	*outside*
therm	*heat*	inter	*between*
collegium	*society or school*	saur	*lizard*
cracy	*rule*	ible	*able to*
dino	*terrible*	pluto	*wealthy*

1. intercollegiate _____

_____

_____

2. dinosaur _____

_____

_____

3. edible _____

_____

_____

4. exothermic _____

_____

_____

5. plutocracy _____

_____

_____

COMMON CORE
STATE STANDARD

L.6.4b

Name_____ Date_____

Greek and Latin Roots

Read the Greek or Latin root and its definition, and then each sentence. Then write the word that best fits the sentence on the line. Use a dictionary for assistance.

1. Root: tempor ("time")
    I didn't like wearing a cast on my broken leg, but the doctor reminded me it was only _____ (temporal, temporary, contemporary) and would be removed soon.

2. Root: **rupt** ("break")
    The explorer watched in amazement as the giant volcano began to _____ (interrupt, rupture, erupt), throwing lava into the air.

3. Root: **vap** ("lack of")
    Terrence did not like the mayor's speech and thought it was overly simple and _____ (evaporation, vapid, vapor) and had little meaning to the people of town.

4. Root: **gran** ("grain")
    During the poor growing season, farmers relied on the crops they had stored in the _____ (granola, granule, granary) during the last harvest.

5. Root: **fac, fic, fact,** or **fect** ("make")
    Kenny was upset when he finally bought the expensive jacket and found out that it had a serious _____ (manufacture, factory, defect).

6. Root: **ann** ("year")
    Our club holds its _____ (annual, anniversary, biannual) meeting in December and June of each year.

Name_____ Date_____

COMMON CORE
STATE STANDARD
L.6.4b

Greek and Latin Affixes and Roots

Identify the Greek or Latin affixes or roots used in each word. Then use a dictionary to help you write a sentence that uses the word correctly.

1. Word: **monolith**

    Affixes and roots: _____

    Example sentence: _____

    _____

2. Word: **pseudonym**

    Affixes and roots: _____

    Example sentence: _____

    _____

3. Word: **centennial**

    Affixes and roots: _____

    Example sentence: _____

    _____

4. Word: **contradict**

    Affixes and roots: _____

    Example sentence: _____

    _____

5. Word: **dialogue**

    Affixes and roots: _____

    Example sentence: _____

    _____

COMMON CORE
STATE STANDARD

L.6.4c

Consult Reference Materials for Pronunciation and Meaning

> **COMMON CORE STATE STANDARD L.6.4c**
> Consult reference materials (e.g., dictionaries, glossaries, thesauruses), both print and digital, to find the pronunciation of a word or determine or clarify its precise meaning or its part of speech.

Explain

Consult reference materials to determine the meanings, parts of speech, and pronunciations of unfamiliar words.

Say: *Sometimes writers or readers need to check a word's meaning or part of speech. Other times, they need to find a more accurate, specific word to use or check a word's pronunciation. They can use a print or digital dictionary, glossary, or thesaurus for these situations. Reference materials, such as a dictionary, often have a pronunciation key that helps you figure out how each word should sound.*

Model

Write the following words on the board and ask the students to look up the meanings, parts of speech, and pronunciations for each word in a dictionary, glossary, or thesaurus.

  principal   principle

Point out that the words *principal* and *principle* are both pronounced the same way (PRIN-sih-pul) even though they are spelled differently. Point out that *principal* as a noun means "the head of a school" and as an adjective means "most important." Point out that *principle* is a noun that means "a moral rule or belief."

Guide Practice

Write these words on the board. Provide the students with online or print dictionaries. Ask a volunteer to look up the meaning, part of speech, and pronunciation of the first word.

  acknowledgment   complicate   peninsula   recollection

Ask: *Were you able to find the meaning, part of speech, and pronunciation of the word* acknowledgment?

Repeat the procedure with the rest of the words. Have the students write the meanings, parts of speech, and pronunciations of the words.

Name_____ Date_____

COMMON CORE
STATE STANDARD
L.6.4c

Consult Reference Materials for Pronunciation

Use **dictionaries** and **glossaries** to determine the **pronunciation** of words. Dictionaries can be found in print or online. Glossaries can be found at the end of many print and digital nonfiction books. Both contain pronunciations and definitions. A pronunciation key will help you interpret the pronunication symbols.

- <u>enjoy</u> *verb* in-ˈjȯi to take pleasure in something
- <u>surprise</u> *noun* sə(r)-ˈprīz an unexpected event, piece of information

Read each word below and use a dictionary to find the correct pronunciations. Be sure to locate and use the dictionary's pronunciation key. Then circle the correct answer to each question.

1. <u>rivalry</u>

Last syllable rhymes with?: **rye**   **bye**   **knee**

2. <u>neutral</u>

First syllable rhymes with?: **new**   **cool**   **know**

3. <u>infinite</u>

Last syllable rhymes with?: **mitt**   **might**   **quite**

4. <u>ambitious</u>

Same *i* sound as middle syllable?: **try**   **bite**   **bit**

5. <u>geyser</u>

First syllable rhymes with?: **me**   **gem**   **pie**

COMMON CORE
STATE STANDARD

L.6.4c

Name_____ Date_____

Consult Reference Materials for Pronunciation

Use a print or online dictionary to look up the words below. Each word has multiple definitions and pronunciations. Choose two different definitions and pronunciations. Fill in the pronunciation and definition, and then write your own sentence that demonstrates the word's meaning.

1. Word: **invalid**

   Pronunciation: _____

   Definition: _____

   Sentence example: _____

   _____

2. Word: **invalid**

   Pronunciation: _____

   Definition: _____

   Sentence example: _____

   _____

3. Word: **moderate**

   Pronunciation: _____

   Definition: _____

   Sentence example: _____

   _____

4. Word: **moderate**

   Pronunciation: _____

   Definition: _____

   Sentence example: _____

   _____

Common Core Language Grade 6 • ©2014 Newmark Learning, LLC

Name_____ Date_____

COMMON CORE
STATE STANDARD
L.6.4c

Consult Reference Materials for Meaning

Use **dictionaries**, **glossaries**, and **thesauruses** to determine the **meaning** of words. Dictionaries and thesauruses can be found in print or online. Glossaries can be found at the end of many print and online nonfiction books. Each contains pronunciation, syllabication, and definitions. Thesauruses provide synonyms and antonyms for words.

- <u>extensive</u> *adjective* ik-ˈsten(t)-siv   large in size or amount
- synonyms: large, substantial, sizable
- antonyms: small, compact, tiny

Read each sentence. Using a print or online dictionary, look up the correct definition of each underlined word and write it on the lines below, including the part of speech.

1. Sam took her coat and pants to the tailors and asked for a few <u>minor</u> alterations.

_____

_____

2. Francois graduated college with a degree in English and a <u>minor</u> in linguistics.

_____

_____

3. If you leave during class, remember to bring your hall pass with you or the hall <u>monitor</u> will assign you detention.

_____

_____

4. We have to <u>monitor</u> the progress of our plants every day for a biology experiment in school.

_____

_____

COMMON CORE
STATE STANDARD
L.6.4c

Name_____ Date_____

Consult Reference Materials for Meaning

Use a dictionary or thesaurus to answer the questions below.

1. Someone just handed you a <u>quire</u>. What did they just give you?

_____

2. Don't forget your <u>salopettes</u> when you're doing this activity.

_____

3. A huge <u>gale</u> just came through the park. What just happened?

_____

4. You woke up in a <u>cantankerous</u> mood. How are you feeling?

_____

5. A <u>borborygmus</u> just came from your friend. What's going on?

_____

6. You've been described as <u>macrosmatic</u>. What are you good at?

_____

7. The library has a collection of <u>incunabula</u>. What does it have?

_____

8. Ignore the <u>argle-bargle</u> over there. What should you ignore?

_____

COMMON CORE
STATE STANDARD
L.6.4c

Name_____ Date_____

Consult Reference Materials for Pronunciation and Meaning

Choose whether to use a dictionary or thesaurus for each problem. Then use that reference material to answer each question.

1. Jessica wants to find two words that mean the opposite of *effective*.

Should she use a dictionary or thesaurus? _____

Two words that have opposite meanings of *effective* are

_____, _____

2. Ernie wants to know two definitions of the word *squash*.

Should he use a dictionary or thesaurus? _____

What are two definitions of *squash*?

a. _____

b. _____

Write a sentence with *squash*, using one of the definitions above:

_____

_____

3. Marcus wants to find two words that mean the same thing as *despise*.

Should he use a dictionary or thesaurus? _____

Two words that have similar meanings of *despise* are

_____, _____

4. Regina is not sure how to pronounce the word *emphasize*.

Should she use a dictionary or thesaurus? _____

The pronunciation of *emphasize* is _____

Write a sentence with *emphasize*: _____

_____

_____

COMMON CORE
STATE STANDARD

L.6.4d

Verify Meanings of Words

> **COMMON CORE STATE STANDARD L.6.4d**
> Verify the preliminary determination of the meaning of a word or phrase (e.g., by checking the inferred meaning in context or in a dictionary).

Explain
Meanings of words can be found by either consulting a dictionary or glossary or by using context clues in writing.

Say: *As readers, we sometimes need to figure out the meaning of new words. We can use context clues in sentences and paragraphs to help us determine meanings of words. We can also look up unfamiliar words in a print or digital dictionary or in a glossary at the end of a book. Even if we use a dictionary, however, we still have to use context clues to determine which definition fits the meaning of the sentence.*

Model
Write the following sentences on the board:

1. *My sister likes to shop for jewelry.*
2. *My sister bought a bracelet at the shop.*

Point out that the word *shop* means something different in each sentence. You can use a dictionary to look up the word *shop*, which has several meanings, but you need to use the context of the sentences to determine the meaning of the word in each sentence.

Guide Practice
Write the word *flood* on the board. Ask a volunteer to look up at least two different meanings for the word. (examples: the overflowing of a body of water; to cover or fill something)

Ask: *Were you able to find at least two different meanings for the word flood?*

Have another volunteer use *flood* in a sentence using the first meaning. Then have students write one more sentence using the second meaning for the word *flood*. Remind them that using context clues is just as important as using a dictionary to determine the meaning of an unfamiliar word in a sentence.

Common Core Language Grade 6 • ©2014 Newmark Learning, LLC

Name_____ Date_____

COMMON CORE
STATE STANDARD
L.6.4d

Verify Meanings of Words

When you are reading, you may come across unfamiliar words. After using context clues, you may still be unsure of a word's meaning. A dictionary or thesaurus is a helpful resource when **verifying the meaning** of an unknown word.

- <u>deteriorate</u> *v* di ˈti(ə)rēəˌrāt   become progressively worse
- <u>omniscient</u> *adj* ämˈni sh ənt   knowing everything

Read the passage. Underline four difficult words or words you do not know. Use a dictionary or thesaurus to look up each word, and write the definitions on the lines below.

The final cumulative math test was approaching, but Liz was reluctant to study for it. She didn't feel inept, but felt adequately prepared to take the exam. She was on the verge of graduating, and didn't want to dwell on trivial exams. With a resigned sigh, Liz cracked open her textbook and commenced studying.

1. _____

   _____

2. _____

   _____

3. _____

   _____

4. _____

   _____

COMMON CORE
STATE STANDARD
L.6.4d

Name_____ Date_____

Verify Meanings of Words

Read each sentence. Choose the correct word from the box and write it on the line. Use a dictionary for assistance.

allusion	illusion	accept
except	capital	capitol

1. Shakespeare's play *Hamlet* contains my favorite literary

   _____ to Greek and Roman mythology.

2. Her friend often gave the _____ that

   everything was perfect.

3. In my geography class, we had to memorize the

   _____ of every U.S. state.

4. The _____ building has been undergoing

   renovations for the past year, so we haven't been able to visit.

5. If I receive the job offer, I will _____.

6. I think all of the paintings in the museum are beautiful

   _____ that one in the corner.

Name_____ Date_____

COMMON CORE
STATE STANDARD
L.6.4d

Verify Meanings of Words

Read each sentence and circle the word that has a similar meaning to the underlined word. Use a dictionary or thesaurus for assistance.

1. Because Megan didn't want to take sides, she remained <u>neutral</u> during the argument.
   a. fair   **b.** unique   **c.** influential   **d.** biased

2. The pages of the old book were <u>brittle</u> and tore easily.
   a. flexible   **b.** vertical   **c.** fragile   **d.** intertwined

3. Mr. Wong was a <u>punctual</u> person and never liked to run behind.
   a. late   **b.** prompt   **c.** clumsy   **d.** lazy

4. The show <u>commenced</u> with the theme song and opening credits.
   a. halted   **b.** dragged on   **c.** presided over   **d.** began

5. The invention of the computer has made older electronics <u>obsolete</u>.
   a. flimsy   **b.** plain   **c.** outdated   **d.** popular

6. The teacher sent the <u>impudent</u> student to the principal's office.
   a. rude   **b.** poor   **c.** notable   **d.** filthy

7. Because it was raining, we had to <u>postpone</u> the picnic.
   a. vent   **b.** plan   **c.** delay   **d.** lengthen

8. Mary tried to <u>persuade</u> me to go with her to the zoo even though I had other plans.
   a. force   **b.** finish   **c.** stop   **d.** coax

9. The freshly baked apple pie gave off an enticing <u>aroma</u>.
   a. sound   **b.** scent   **c.** warmness   **d.** delicious

10. After playing the game for a few days, it lost its <u>novelty</u>, and we became bored with it.
    a. variety   **b.** decency   **c.** difficulty   **d.** newness

COMMON CORE
STATE STANDARD

L.6.5a

Interpret Figures of Speech

COMMON CORE STATE STANDARD L.6.5a
Interpret figures of speech (e.g., personification) in context

Explain
Writers often use figures of speech to create interesting, surprising images with their words. Simile, metaphor, personification, and irony are popular examples of figures of speech.

Say: *Figures of speech include simile, metaphor, personification, and irony. A simile is a comparison between two unlike things that uses* like *or* as. *A metaphor is a direct comparison between unlike things. Personification means assigning human characteristics or abilities to an animal or object. Irony means using words or ideas that are different from what is expected or what usually happens.*

Model
Write the following paragraph on the board.

> *The wind whispered to itself as it blew through the trees. With each gust, the leaves danced across the forest floor. The clear stream laughed quietly as it flowed over the stones.*

Point out that these sentences contain three examples of personification: the writer says that the wind whispers, the leaves dance, and the stream laughs. Whispering, dancing, and laughing are things humans do, not objects. The writer chooses to use these figures of speech to help readers "hear" and "see" the scene by giving the wind, leaves, and stream human qualities.

Guide Practice
Write the following sentences on the board. Ask a volunteer to find and identify the figures of speech contained in the first sentence.

1. *The master chef burned his toast this morning.* (saying a master chef failed at a simple cooking task is an example of irony)
2. *The Internet is a treasure chest of information.* (comparing the Internet and a treasure chest is a metaphor)

Ask: *Were you able to determine that a master chef failing at a simple cooking task is an example of irony?*

Repeat the procedure with the remaining sentence. Have the students find and identify the figures of speech in the remaining sentence. Remind them that figures of speech make writing more exciting, interesting, and surprising.

Common Core Language Grade 6 • ©2014 Newmark Learning, LLC

Name_____ Date_____

COMMON CORE
STATE STANDARD
L.6.5a

Interpret Figures of Speech

Writers use **figures of speech** to make their writing exciting, interesting, and surprising. Figures of speech include similes, metaphors, personification, and irony.

Figure of Speech	Definition	Example
simile	comparison using like or as	*He is as tough as nails.*
metaphor	direct comparison between unlike things	*She has a heart of gold.*
personification	assigning human traits or qualities to non-human things	*Time crawled slowly.*
irony	using words to mean the opposite of their literal definition	*The fire station burned down.*

Circle the correct figure of speech used in each sentence. Then on the lines below, explain the meaning of each sentence.

1. **My computer doesn't like me.**

    Type of figure of speech: simile metaphor personification irony

    Meaning of sentence: _____

    _____

2. **The newborn baby was as pretty as a picture.**

    Type of figure of speech: simile metaphor personification irony

    Meaning of figure of speech: _____

    _____

3. **The car mechanic needed a ride since his car wouldn't start.**

    Type of figure of speech: simile metaphor personification irony

    Meaning of figure of speech: _____

    _____

4. **The heart is the body's engine.**

    Type of figure of speech: simile metaphor personification irony

    Meaning of figure of speech: _____

    _____

COMMON CORE
STATE STANDARD
L.6.5a

Name_____ Date_____

Interpret Figures of Speech

Read each sentence. Underline examples of personification. Then circle the object being personified.

1. The angry ocean threw huge waves against the shore.

2. The squirrel enjoyed a take-out dinner of acorns and birdseed.

3. The mailbox opened its mouth and gobbled up the letters.

4. The hateful lightning flashed a warning to the hikers.

5. I looked up at the night sky and saw a star wink at me.

Complete each sentence with a simile or metaphor.

6. The crying child was as loud as _____

_____

7. The toy boat sank like _____

_____

8. Suzann's pet dog is _____

_____

9. I tried to carry the book bag but it was _____

_____

10. The storm tossed the boat like _____

_____

Name_____ Date_____

COMMON CORE
STATE STANDARD
L.6.5a

Interpret Figures of Speech

Circle the correct figure of speech used in each sentence. Then on the lines below, explain the meaning of each sentence.

1. **The rain was tap-dancing on the roof.**

   Type of figure of speech: simile metaphor personification irony

   Meaning: _____

   _____

2. **I studied all week for a Spanish test but then I remembered it was an English test!**

   Type of figure of speech: simile metaphor personification irony

   Meaning: _____

   _____

3. **When Jeremy took my hat, I was as angry as a hornet.**

   Type of figure of speech: simile metaphor personification irony

   Meaning: _____

   _____

4. **From high up in the airplane, the busy streets below were lines of ants.**

   Type of figure of speech: simile metaphor personification irony

   Meaning: _____

   _____

5. **The flowers in the garden smiled at me in the morning.**

   Type of figure of speech: simile metaphor personification irony

   Meaning: _____

   _____

6. **Jimmy thought that class was as boring as watching paint dry.**

   Type of figure of speech: simile metaphor personification irony

   Meaning: _____

   _____

COMMON CORE
STATE STANDARD
L.6.5b

Word Relationships

> **COMMON CORE STATE STANDARD L.6.5b**
> Use the relationship between particular words (e.g., cause/effect, part/whole, item/category) to better understand each of the words.

Explain
The relationship between particular words provides clues to understanding the meanings.

Say: *The particular way in which writing is organized helps signal relationships between words, which provides context clues to their meanings. A cause-and-effect relationship indicates whether a word is a part of an event or the reason behind it. A part-and-whole relationship indicates that a word is a piece or element of something bigger. An item-and-category relationship indicates that a word's meaning is related to other words in the same category.*

Model
Write the following on the board:

1. *fall–bruise*
2. *toe–foot*
3. *banana–fruit*

Point out the relationships between the pairs of words: cause/effect, part/whole, item/category.

Guide Practice
Write the following on the board. Ask a volunteer to use the first word pair in a cause-and-effect sentence.

1. *bridge–detour*
2. *dungeon–castle*
3. *harmonica–instrument*

Ask: *Does this sentence demonstrate the relationship between the words?*

Repeat the procedure with the second pair (part/whole) and third (item/category). Have students write one sentence demonstrating each of the above word relationships in their notebooks. Remind them that the relationship between particular words provides clues to understanding them.

Name_____ Date_____

Common Core State Standard
L.6.5b

Word Relationships—Cause/Effect

Using certain words in a sentence can imply different **word relationships**. There are signal words that you can look for in a sentence that indicate a cause-and-effect relationship. With a cause-and-effect word relationship, one word in each pair is the cause of another word.

Signal Words: *if, then, because, now that, since, so, despite, before, after*

Example: *Because* of the heavy rain, the streets were flooded. (*heavy rain* is the cause, and *flooded* is the effect)

Complete each sentence using signal words to indicate a cause-and-effect word relationship.

1. My mom's hat blew away _____

_____

2. The little boy was so bashful _____

_____

3. Sara wants to work for NASA _____

_____

4. _____

_____, the roses won't die in

the harsh winter.

5. _____

_____, he still held a grudge.

COMMON CORE
STATE STANDARD
L.6.5b

Name_____ Date_____

Word Relationships—Cause/Effect

Read each incomplete analogy below. Think about the cause-and-effect relationship the words have with each other, and complete each analogy.

1. *Sun* is to *daytime* as *moon* is to _____.

2. *Joke* is to *laughter* as *tragedy* is to _____.

3. *Careless* is to *accident* as *careful* is to _____.

4. *Flame* is to *wildfire* as *snowflake* is to _____.

5. *Sunrise* is to *dawn* as *sunset* is to _____.

Read the words below. Then draw a line to match each cause on the left with an effect on the right.

6. tired   **a.** gossip

7. scandal   **b.** reaction

8. explanation   **c.** sleep

9. action   **d.** compromise

10. negotiation   **e.** understanding

Common Core Language Grade 6 • ©2014 Newmark Learning, LLC

Name_____ Date_____

COMMON CORE
STATE STANDARD
L.6.5b

Word Relationships—Part/Whole

A **part-and-whole relationship** indicates that one word in each pair is part of the other word. Relationships between particular words provide clues to word meanings and function.

- *Books* are to *libraries* as *paintings* are to *museums*.
- *Fingers* are to *hands* as *toes* are to *feet*.

Read each incomplete analogy below. Think about the part-to-whole relationship the words have with each other, and complete each analogy.

1. *Leaf* is to *tree* as *petal* is to _____.

2. *City* is to *state* as *state* is to _____.

3. *Second* is to *minute* as *minute* is to _____.

4. *Violinist* is to *orchestra* as *catcher* is to _____.

5. *Letter* is to *word* as *word* is to _____.

6. *Palm* is to *hand* as *knuckle* is to _____.

7. *Flowers* are to *garden* as *trees* are to _____.

8. *Lion* is to *pride* as *wolf* is to _____.

COMMON CORE
STATE STANDARD
L.6.5b

Name_____ Date_____

Word Relationships—Part/Whole

Read the list of words. Then circle the part that does not belong with each bold word.

1. **fish**   gills   lungs   scales

2. **clock**   second   cogs   pendulum

3. **painting**   brushes   pens   easel

4. **salad**   tomato   lettuce   ice

5. **continents**   Africa   Canada   Asia

On the lines below, write your own part/whole analogies.

6. _____

_____

7. _____

_____

8. _____

_____

Common Core Language Grade 6 • ©2014 Newmark Learning, LLC

Name_____ Date_____

COMMON CORE
STATE STANDARD
L.6.5b

Word Relationships—Item/Category

> An **item-and-category relationship** indicates that a word's meaning is related to other words in the same category.
>
> - *Car* is to *vehicle* as *yacht* is to *boat*.
>   (*Car* is a type of vehicle, and *yacht* is a type of boat.)
> - *Apple* is to *fruit* as *carrot* is to *vegetable*.

Read each sentence. Decide what category the underlined words are in, based on the item-and-category relationships.

1. Farra enjoys <u>jazz</u> and <u>tap</u>, so she has started learning <u>ballet</u>.

   _____

2. Jackie chose a navy <u>jacket</u> and crimson <u>scarf</u>.

   _____

3. Mom is making a salad of <u>strawberries</u> and <u>cantaloupe</u>.

   _____

4. We're having <u>burgers</u> and <u>frankfurters</u> at the team party.

   _____

5. The table is <u>oak</u> and the picture frame is <u>mahogany</u>.

   _____

6. She took <u>piano</u> and <u>violin</u> lessons every week after school.

   _____

COMMON CORE
STATE STANDARD
L.6.5b

Name_____ Date_____

Word Relationships—Item/Category

Read each sentence. Decide what category the underlined words are in, based on the item-and-category relationships.

1. Grandpa always plants <u>lavender</u> near his <u>roses</u>.

_____

2. Aunt Alice is making pillows of <u>silk</u> and <u>rayon</u>.

_____

3. Frances has a <u>magazine</u> today, but her sister is enjoying a <u>novel</u>.

_____

4. Would you like some <u>cake</u> or a <u>pastry</u>?

_____

Read the words below. Then draw a line to match each item on the left with a category on the right.

5. Argentina	**a.** language
6. German	**b.** stone
7. south	**c.** jewelry
8. marble	**d.** tool
9. earrings	**e.** country
10. wrench	**f.** direction

Name_____ Date_____

COMMON CORE
STATE STANDARD
L.6.5b

Word Relationships

Read the following sentences. Decide whether they include cause-and-effect, part-and-whole, or item-and-category relationships.

1. Last week we took a test about typhoons and blizzards.

_____

2. Due to the blindfold, Rita could not see the piñata when she tried to hit it. _____

3. Ingrid has learned the piano piece, so she will play in a recital.

_____

4. The lenses on the binoculars are scratched and dirty.

_____

5. Each stanza in this poem contains four lines.

_____

6. The robot's head began to spin and its eyes began to flash.

_____

7. The computer is defective, so we will return it to the store.

_____

8. Lemurs, jaguars, and gorillas all live in rainforests.

_____

COMMON CORE
STATE STANDARD
L.6.5c

Distinguish Connotations

> **COMMON CORE STATE STANDARD L.6.5c**
>
> Distinguish among the connotations (associations) of words with similar denotations (definitions) (e.g., *stingy, scrimping, economical, unwasteful, thrifty*).

Explain

Tell students that most words have more than one meaning. There are two types of meanings—denotation is a word's dictionary definition, but its connotation is the association or emotional value people give to it. Connotations have shades of meaning so you can decide how to use them.

Say: *Certain words, even though they mean almost the same thing, have different connotations. For example, think about a house and then think about a home. What is the difference? A house is just a building, but a home is a secure place where you are loved and cared for. That's the difference between denotation and connotation.*

Model

Explain that words can have positive, negative, or neutral connotations.

Positive: *cabin*   Neutral: *shelter*   Negative: *shack*

Point out that not all words have all three connotations and that the connotation depends upon the context and/or culture in which it is used. Tell students that writers and speakers must be sure they know a word's connotative meanings before using it.

Guide Practice

Write the following sentences on the board. Ask a volunteer to switch the word *child* in the first sentence from a neutral word to a similar word with negative connotation and then to a positive connotation.

1. *Dulcie's* child *is a legend in their neighborhood.*
   (Dulcie's *brat* is a legend in their neighborhood.)
   (Dulcie's *whiz kid* is a legend in their neighborhood.)
2. *We had lunch at a little restaurant on Liberty Street.*

Ask: *How does the change affect the rest of the sentence?*

Repeat the procedure with the second sentence. Then have the students tell how the connotation of each replacement changes the sentence. Remind them that they must understand the connotation of a word before using it when writing or speaking.

Name_____ Date_____

COMMON CORE
STATE STANDARD
L.6.5c

Distinguish Connotations

> The **connotation** of a word is the ideas or feelings associated with that word. These are not part of a word's definition ("denotation"). A word's connotation can be neutral, positive, or negative.
>
> - <u>hungry</u> (neutral) or <u>starving</u> (negative)
> - <u>thin</u> (neutral) or <u>slender</u> (positive) or <u>skinny</u> (negative)

Using a dictionary, fill in the denotation for each pair of words below. Then describe whether each word has a positive, negative, or neutral connotation.

Word	Denotation	Connotation
1. thoughtful		
brooding		
2. influential		
controlling		
3. smart		
brilliant		

COMMON CORE
STATE STANDARD
L.6.5c

Name_____ Date_____

Distinguish Connotations

Read the following words. Then write whether each word has a positive, negative, or neutral connotation. Use a dictionary for assistance.

1. ambitious _____

2. irritating _____

3. adult _____

4. thought _____

5. pandemonium _____

Write a sentence using each word below. Your sentence should indicate whether each word has a positive, negative, or neutral connotation.

6. economical

_____

_____

7. stingy

_____

_____

8. frugal

_____

_____

Common Core Language Grade 6 • ©2014 Newmark Learning, LLC

Name_____ Date_____

COMMON CORE
STATE STANDARD
L.6.5c

Distinguish Connotations

Write two descriptions, one positive and one negative, using the following scenario.

Luke cooked a large dinner for Rosa. Seafood on rice was the main dish. He cooked a side dish of vegetables, as well as dessert.

1. Describe the meal using words that make it sound tempting and delicious.

_____

_____

_____

_____

_____

_____

2. Describe the meal using words that make it sound very unappealing.

_____

_____

_____

_____

_____

_____

How to Use the Practice Assessments

The quick practice assessments provided in this section are designed for easy implementation in any classroom. They can be used in several different ways. You may wish to administer a conventions assessment and a vocabulary assessment together. They may also be used individually as an informal assessment tool throughout the year. Use the following charts for item analysis and scoring.

Student Name:

Conventions	Date	Item	Standard	✔=0 X=1	Total
Assessment 1		1	**L.6.1a:** Ensure that pronouns are in the proper case (subjective, objective, possessive). **L.6.1d:** Recognize and correct vague pronouns (i.e., ones with unclear or ambiguous antecedents).		
		2	**L.6.1b:** Use intensive pronouns (e.g., *myself, ourselves*).		
		3	**L.6.2a:** Use punctuation (commas, parentheses, dashes) to set off nonrestrictive/parenthetical elements.		
		4	**L.6.3a:** Vary sentence patterns for meaning, reader/listener interest, and style.		
		5	**L.6.1c:** Recognize and correct inappropriate shifts in pronoun number and person.		
		6	**L.6.1a:** Ensure that pronouns are in the proper case (subjective, objective, possessive). **L.6.2b:** Spell correctly.		
Assessment 2		1	**L.6.2b:** Spell correctly.		
		2	**L.6.2a:** Use punctuation (commas, parentheses, dashes) to set off nonrestrictive/parenthetical elements.		
		3	**L.6.3a:** Vary sentence patterns for meaning, reader/listener interest, and style.		
		4	**L.6.3a:** Vary sentence patterns for meaning, reader/listener interest, and style.		
		5	**L.6.2b:** Spell correctly.		
		6	**L.6.1a:** Ensure that pronouns are in the proper case (subjective, objective, possessive).		

Student Name:

Conventions	Date	Item	Standard	✔=0 X=1	Total
Assessment 3		1	**L.6.1d:** Recognize and correct vague pronouns (i.e., ones with unclear or ambiguous antecedents).		
		2	**L.6.2a:** Use punctuation (commas, parentheses, dashes) to set off nonrestrictive/parenthetical elements.		
		3	**L.6.2b:** Spell correctly.		
		4	**L.6.1e:** Recognize variations from standard English in their own and others' writing and speaking, and identify and use strategies to improve expression in conventional language.		
		5	**L.6.2b:** Spell correctly.		
		6	**L.6.3b:** Maintain consistency in style and tone.		
Assessment 4		1	**L.6.2a:** Use punctuation (commas, parentheses, dashes) to set off nonrestrictive/parenthetical elements.		
		2	**L.6.2b:** Spell correctly.		
		3	**L.6.1b:** Use intensive pronouns (e.g., *myself, ourselves*).		
		4	**L.6.2a:** Use punctuation (commas, parentheses, dashes) to set off nonrestrictive/parenthetical elements.		
		5	**L.6.1a:** Ensure that pronouns are in the proper case (subjective, objective, possessive).		
Assessment 5		1	**L.6.2b:** Spell correctly.		
		2	**L.6.1c:** Recognize and correct inappropriate shifts in pronoun number and person.		
		3	**L.6.1e:** Recognize variations from standard English in their own and others' writing and speaking, and identify and use strategies to improve expression in conventional language.		
		4	**L.6.1a:** Ensure that pronouns are in the proper case (subjective, objective, possessive).		
		5	**L.6.1d:** Recognize and correct vague pronouns (i.e., ones with unclear or ambiguous antecedents).		

Student Name:

Vocabulary	Date	Item	Standard	✔=0 X=1	Total
Assessment 1		1	**L.6.4c:** Consult reference materials (e.g., dictionaries, glossaries, thesauruses), both print and digital, to find the pronunciation of a word or determine or clarify its precise meaning or its part of speech.		
		2	**L.6.4d:** Verify the preliminary determination of the meaning of a word or phrase (e.g., by checking the inferred meaning in context or in a dictionary).		
		3	**L.6.4a:** Use context (e.g., the overall meaning of a sentence or paragraph; a word's position or function in a sentence) as a clue to the meaning of a word or phrase.		
		4	**L.6.4d:** Verify the preliminary determination of the meaning of a word or phrase (e.g., by checking the inferred meaning in context or in a dictionary).		
		5	**L.6.4c:** Consult reference materials (e.g., dictionaries, glossaries, thesauruses), both print and digital, to find the pronunciation of a word or determine or clarify its precise meaning or its part of speech.		
		6	**L.6.4c:** Consult reference materials (e.g., dictionaries, glossaries, thesauruses), both print and digital, to find the pronunciation of a word or determine or clarify its precise meaning or its part of speech.		
Assessment 2		1	**L.6.4c:** Consult reference materials (e.g., dictionaries, glossaries, thesauruses), both print and digital, to find the pronunciation of a word or determine or clarify its precise meaning or its part of speech.		
		2	**L.6.4c:** Consult reference materials (e.g., dictionaries, glossaries, thesauruses), both print and digital, to find the pronunciation of a word or determine or clarify its precise meaning or its part of speech.		
		3	**L.6.4c:** Consult reference materials (e.g., dictionaries, glossaries, thesauruses), both print and digital, to find the pronunciation of a word or determine or clarify its precise meaning or its part of speech.		
		4	**L.6.4d:** Verify the preliminary determination of the meaning of a word or phrase (e.g., by checking the inferred meaning in context or in a dictionary).		
		5	**L.6.4d:** Verify the preliminary determination of the meaning of a word or phrase (e.g., by checking the inferred meaning in context or in a dictionary).		

Student Name:

Vocabulary	Date	Item	Standard	✓=0 X=1	Total
Assessment 3		1	**L.6.4a:** Use context (e.g., the overall meaning of a sentence or paragraph; a word's position or function in a sentence) as a clue to the meaning of a word or phrase.		
		2	**L.6.3b:** Maintain consistency in style and tone.		
		3	**L.6.3b:** Maintain consistency in style and tone.		
		4	**L.6.1b:** Use intensive pronouns (e.g., *myself, ourselves*).		
		5	**L.6.2b:** Spell correctly.		
Assessment 4		1	**L.6.4d:** Verify the preliminary determination of the meaning of a word or phrase (e.g., by checking the inferred meaning in context or in a dictionary).		
		2	**L.6.4c:** Consult reference materials (e.g., dictionaries, glossaries, thesauruses), both print and digital, to find the pronunciation of a word or determine or clarify its precise meaning or its part of speech.		
		3	**L.6.4b:** Use common, grade-appropriate Greek or Latin affixes and roots as clues to the meaning of a word (e.g., *audience, auditory, audible*).		
		4	**L.6.5c:** Distinguish among the connotations (associations) of words with similar denotations (definitions) (e.g., *stingy, scrimping, economical, unwasteful, thrifty*).		
		5	**L.6.4c:** Consult reference materials (e.g., dictionaries, glossaries, thesauruses), both print and digital, to find the pronunciation of a word or determine or clarify its precise meaning or its part of speech.		
Assessment 5		1	**L.6.4a:** Use context (e.g., the overall meaning of a sentence or paragraph; a word's position or function in a sentence) as a clue to the meaning of a word or phrase.		
		2	**L.6.5a:** Interpret figures of speech (e.g., personification) in context.		
		3	**L.6.5a:** Interpret figures of speech (e.g., personification) in context.		
		4	**L.6.5b:** Use the relationship between particular words (e.g., cause/effect, part/whole, item/category) to better understand each of the words.		
		5	**L.6.5c:** Distinguish among the connotations (associations) of words with similar denotations (definitions) (e.g., *stingy, scrimping, economical, unwasteful, thrifty*).		

COMMON CORE
STATE STANDARDS

L.6.1–
L.6.3

Name_____ Date_____

Read the passage. Then choose the correct form of the underlined sentence.

Lydia put her hand in front of her mouth to hide her grin. Her little brother, Carter, was hopping in place. <u>[1] Now that they were actually standing outside the fire station, they was beside himself with exsitement.</u>

<u>[2] The door opened, and Uncle Rick stepped outside himself. [3] He was wearing his firefighter uniform a blue shirt and black pants and he was grinning, too.</u> "Welcome to Station 12!" he said, hugging them both. "Are you ready for the grand tour?" <u>[4] Uncle Rick held the door open. They stepped inside. [5] "I want you to meet my friends, she's in the kitchen right now," said Uncle Rick as he lead them down a hall.</u>

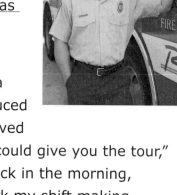

"Hi, I'm Maria," said a firefighter as she wiped a table. Other firefighters, who Uncle Rick introduced as Joe and Kurt, were washing dishes. They waved to the visitors. "I took Rick's job tonight so he could give you the tour," Maria said to Lydia and Carter. "He'll pay me back in the morning, though. <u>[6] Him has to get up super erly and work my shift making breakfast." Lydia hid her mouth again, grinning. Uncle Rick was a terrible cook!</u>

1. Ⓐ Now that they were actually standing outside the fire station, him was beside himself with excitment.

   Ⓑ Now that they were actually standing outside the fire station, they were beside themselves with excitement.

   Ⓒ Now that she was actually standing outside the fire station, he were beside himself with excitemint.

   Ⓓ No change

106

Name_____ Date_____

Common Core
State Standards
L.6.1–
L.6.3

2. Ⓐ The door opened, and himself Uncle Rick stepped outside.

   Ⓑ The door opened himself, and Uncle Rick stepped outside.

   Ⓒ The door opened, and Uncle Rick himself stepped outside.

   Ⓓ No change

3. Ⓐ He was wearing his firefighter uniform—a blue shirt and black pants—and he was grinning, too.

   Ⓑ He was wearing, his firefighter uniform a blue shirt and black pants, and he was grinning, too.

   Ⓒ He was wearing his firefighter uniform, a blue shirt, and black pants, and he was grinning, too.

   Ⓓ No change

4. Ⓐ Uncle Rick held the door open, and they stepped inside.

   Ⓑ Uncle Rick held the door open, as they stepped inside.

   Ⓒ Uncle Rick held the door open, they stepped inside.

   Ⓓ No change

5. Ⓐ "They want you to meet my friends, they're in the kitchen right now," said Uncle Rick as he lead them down a hall.

   Ⓑ "I want you to meet my friends, I'm in the kitchen right now," said Uncle Rick as he lead herself down a hall.

   Ⓒ "I want you to meet my friends. They're in the kitchen right now," said Uncle Rick as he led them down a hall.

   Ⓓ No change

6. Ⓐ He has to get up super early and work my's shift making breakfast.

   Ⓑ He has to get up super early and work my shift making breakfast.

   Ⓒ Him has to get up super erly and work myself's shift making breakfast.

   Ⓓ No change

Common Core
State Standards
L.6.1–
L.6.3

Name_____ Date_____

Read the passage. Then choose the correct form of the underlined sentence.

¹ Sean had always dreamed of becoming a profesional basketball player. ² He first stepped onto the court when he began playing in his school's bitty league, which is for the youngest students and never looked back. Growing up, he worked on his game as much as he possibly could. ³ He practiced constantly, and even when he had no one to practice with. ⁴ Sean went to high school. He himself became the team's star player. ⁵ Thanks to his skill and determanation, Sean outshone nearly everyone else and earned a chance to play college basketball. Although he didn't stand out as much from other players in college, Sean was still good enough to catch the attention of some important people in the pro basketball world. As soon as he graduated, Sean got a call from the managers of a big-time pro team. ⁶ They wanted him to be a part of they team! His dream had come true!

1.
- Ⓐ Sean had always dreamed of becoming a profescional basketball player.
- Ⓑ Sean had always dreamed of becoming a professional basketball player.
- Ⓒ Sean had always dreamed of becoming a profeccional basketball player.
- Ⓓ no change

2.
- Ⓐ He first stepped onto the court when he began playing in his school's bitty league, which is for the youngest students, and never looked back.
- Ⓑ He first stepped onto the court when he began playing in his school's bitty league which is for the youngest students, and never looked back.
- Ⓒ He first stepped onto the court when he began playing in his school's bitty league which is for the youngest students and never looked back.
- Ⓓ no change

Common Core Language Grade 6 • ©2014 Newmark Learning, LLC

COMMON CORE
STATE STANDARDS
L.6.1–
L.6.3

Name_____ Date_____

3. Ⓐ He practiced constantly, even, when he had no one, to practice with.

   Ⓑ He practiced constantly. Even when he had no one to practice with.

   Ⓒ He practiced constantly, even when he had no one to practice with.

   Ⓓ no change

4. Ⓐ When Sean went to high school, he quickly became the team's star player.

   Ⓑ Sean went to high school, he quickly became the team's star player.

   Ⓒ When Sean, went to high school, he quickly became the team's star player.

   Ⓓ no change

5. Ⓐ Thanks to his skill and determination, Sean outshown nearly everyone else and earned a chance to play college basketball.

   Ⓑ Thanks to his skill and determanation, Sean outshown nearly everyone else and earned a chance to play college basketball.

   Ⓒ Thanks to his skill and determination, Sean outshone nearly everyone else and earned a chance to play college basketball.

   Ⓓ no change

6. Ⓐ They wanted him to be a part of them team.

   Ⓑ They wanted him to be a part of their team.

   Ⓒ They wanted him to be a part of theirs team.

   Ⓓ no change

COMMON CORE
STATE STANDARDS

L.6.1–
L.6.3

Name_____ Date_____

Read the passage. Then choose the correct form of the underlined sentence.

¹ Sunee and Arlie had planned to walk to school so they could get there early, but as usual she was late. ² The girls ended up running to the bus stop, yelling for the driver to wait, and crumpling into their seats exhausted.

"Why are you always late?" Sunee asked her friend crossly.

"Why are you always grouchy?" said Arlie.

"Because you are always late!" Sunee replied.

By the time they got to school, Sunee had cooled down. ³ She didn't want to loose her best friend.

⁴ "May I be of assistance in supporting you?" she asked Arlie. "I know you don't mean to be late."

⁵ "Of coarse I don't," said Arlie. "Maybe you can help me. What do you do to get out on time?"

"Let's make a list," Sunee suggested. "I'll write down the things I do the night before and the things I do in the morning. Then we'll try to make it work for you. ⁶ You won't have to fall through it all on your own."

1. Ⓐ Sunee and Arlie, planned to walk to school, so they could get there early, but as usual she was late.

   Ⓑ Sunee and Arlie had planned to walk to school so they could get there early, but as usual Arlie was late.

   Ⓒ Sunee and Arlie were planning to walk to school, so they got there early, but as usual she was late.

   Ⓓ No change

Common Core Language Grade 6 • ©2014 Newmark Learning, LLC

Name_____ Date_____

2. Ⓐ The girls ended up running to the bus stop; yelling for the driver to wait; and crumpling into their seats exhausted.

   Ⓑ The girls ended up running to the bus stop, yelling for the driver to wait and crumpling into their seats exhuasted.

   Ⓒ The girls ran to the bus stop yelling for the driver to wait and crumpling into their seats exhausted.

   Ⓓ No change

3. Ⓐ She didn't want to lose her best friend.

   Ⓑ She didn't want to loose her best freind.

   Ⓒ She didn't want to lose her best freind.

   Ⓓ No change

4. Ⓐ "May I be of help in supporting you?"

   Ⓑ "May I be of assistance in instructing you?"

   Ⓒ "Is there something I can do to help you?"

   Ⓓ No change

5. Ⓐ "Of coarse I do not," said Arlie.

   Ⓑ "Of course I don't," said Arlie.

   Ⓒ "Of coarse I don't, said Arlie."

   Ⓓ No change

6. Ⓐ You won't have to stumble through it all on your own.

   Ⓑ You won't have to slip through it all on your own.

   Ⓒ You won't have to topple through it all on your own.

   Ⓓ No change

COMMON CORE
STATE STANDARDS
L.6.1–
L.6.3

Name_____ Date_____

Read the passage. Then choose the correct form of the underlined sentence.

When the final school bell rang at the end of the day on Monday afternoon, Laura, Devin, and Quinn raced to the auditorium. [1] Their goal was to be the first students to arrive at the auditions for the upcoming school play that the drama teacher, Mr. Williams, was holding.

This year's spring play was a comedy about a wedding day on which everything seems to go wrong. The reason Laura, Devin, and Quinn were anxious to get to the auditions first was that they each had a part they wanted to play. [2] Quinn wanted to play Rachel, the bewilldered bride and star of the producion. [3] Laura hoped to land the part of Rachel's frantic mother, Dolores, for her. [4] Devin, meanwhile, was looking to play Roger. The suddenly cold-footed groom.

All three took their turns auditioning for the parts they wanted and did their best to win over Mr. Williams. [5] When the auditions were over, Mr. Williams announced he would consider everything he saw and post him final cast list at the end of the week. To Laura, Devin, and Quinn, the end of the week seemed as if it was a lifetime away. "What will we do with ourselves until then?" Laura asked nervously.

1. Ⓐ Their goal was to be the first students to arrive at the auditions for the upcoming school play that the drama teacher, Mr. Williams was holding.

Ⓑ Their goal was to be the first students to arrive at the auditions for the upcoming school play that the drama teacher Mr. Williams, was holding.

Ⓒ Their goal was to be the first students to arrive at the auditions for the upcoming school play that the drama teacher Mr. Williams was holding.

Ⓓ no change

Name_____ Date_____

COMMON CORE
STATE STANDARDS
L.6.1–
L.6.3

2. Ⓐ Quinn wanted to play Rachel, the bewilldered bride and star of the production.

Ⓑ Quinn wanted to play Rachel, the bewildered bride and star of the production.

Ⓒ Quinn wanted to play Rachel, the bewildered bride and star of the producion.

Ⓓ no change

---

3. Ⓐ Laura herself hoped to land the part of Rachel's frantic mother, Dolores.

Ⓑ Laura ourself hoped to land the part of Rachel's frantic mother, Dolores.

Ⓒ Laura myself hoped to land the part of Rachel's frantic mother, Dolores.

Ⓓ no change

---

4. Ⓐ Devin, meanwhile, was looking to play Roger the suddenly, cold-footed groom.

Ⓑ Devin meanwhile, was looking to play Roger, the suddenly cold-footed groom.

Ⓒ Devin, meanwhile, was looking to play Roger, the suddenly cold-footed groom.

Ⓓ no change

---

5. Ⓐ When the auditions were over, Mr. Williams announced he would consider everything his saw and post him final cast list at the end of the week.

Ⓑ When the auditions were over, Mr. Williams announced he would consider everything him saw and post his final cast list at the end of the week.

Ⓒ When the auditions were over, Mr. Williams announced he would consider everything he saw and post his final cast list at the end of the week.

Ⓓ no change

Common Core
State Standards

L.6.1–
L.6.3

Name_____ Date_____

Read the following passage. Rewrite the passage on the lines below, correcting the grammatical errors.

Amelia and Cosmo

Amelia Marin sat down on a bench under a tree in Harris Hill Park. She took her guitar from it's case and began to strum softly. Lost in her music, she was surprised to feel something wet touch her hand. Opening her eyes, she saw a large dog sitting on the walkway in front of her. She put out her hand and spoke softly to the animal, but it just looked at her and wagged its tail. Then he bended down and nudged a sturdy stick that laid in front of him. He gave a hopeful woof and nudged the stick again.

"Oh, I see. You want me to throw the stick?" asked Amelia. She looked around for someone the dog might of came with. She saw a teenage girl approaching.

"Him and me were going to play," she said. She was a little disappointed.

"Well, if you throw a stick for Cosmo, you could be here for hours. He never knows when to stop!" said the girl.

_____

_____

_____

_____

_____

Common Core Language Grade 6 • ©2014 Newmark Learning, LLC

Name_____ Date_____

COMMON CORE
STATE STANDARDS
L.6.1–
L.6.3

_____

_____

_____

_____

_____

_____

_____

_____

_____

_____

_____

_____

Name_____ Date_____

Common Core
State Standards

L.6.4–
L.6.6

Name_____ Date_____

Read the following dictionary entries. Then use them to answer the following questions.

> **1. content** kən-ˈtent *adj.* 1. pleased and satisfied; *v.* 1. to appease
>
> someone; 2. to limit oneself
>
> **2. content** ˈkän-ˌtent *n.* 1. something contained; 2. substance or
>
> meaning; 3. matter dealt with in a field of study
>
> **3. contention** kən-ˈten-shən *n.* 1. heated
>
> disagreement; 2. a point maintained
>
> in a debate or argument; 3. rivalry

1. **Which part of speech for the word *content* means substance or meaning?**

Ⓐ adjective

Ⓑ verb

Ⓒ noun

Ⓓ adverb

_____

2. **How many parts of speech are listed for *content* in the dictionary entry?**

Ⓐ one

Ⓑ two

Ⓒ three

Ⓓ four

Common Core Language Grade 6 • ©2014 Newmark Learning, LLC

Name_____ Date_____

3. **Which sentence includes the word *content* used as a noun?**

Ⓐ She was content with the way the book ended.

Ⓑ Nathan was content to stay home.

Ⓒ Wendy skimmed the page for its content.

Ⓓ Marcus was easily contented by the simple things in life.

4. **Read the sentence below. Which meaning of *content* is used in the sentence?**

The hungry travelers felt content after their meal.

Ⓐ pleased and satisfied

Ⓑ to limit oneself

Ⓒ something contained

Ⓓ substance or meaning

5. **Which sentence uses the second definition of *contention*?**

Ⓐ There has been too much contention in this family for the past ten years.

Ⓑ They are both in contention for the silver medal.

Ⓒ It is his contention that the new legislation will benefit only a small number of people.

Ⓓ The boxing champion is now out of contention of the world title.

6. **Which word below is NOT a synonym for the first definition of *contention*?**

Ⓐ *debate*

Ⓑ *consensus*

Ⓒ *argument*

Ⓓ *dispute*

Common Core State Standards
L.6.4–
L.6.6

Name______________________________ Date________

competition

Read the thesaurus entry. Then use it to answer the questions that follow.

1. ferocious *adj.* fə-ˈrō-shəs 1. fierce, cruel, or violent; 2. extremely intense or unpleasant

Derivatives: ferociously (*adv*), ferociousness (*n*)

1. Which word is a synonym of the first definition of *ferocious*?

Ⓐ savage
Ⓑ vain
Ⓒ afraid
Ⓓ organized

2. Which word is an antonym of the first definition of *ferocious*?

Ⓐ honest
Ⓑ insightful
Ⓒ tender
Ⓓ radiant

3. Which sentence uses a synonym of *ferocious*?

Ⓐ He yelled at the animal in an inhumane way.
Ⓑ The warm weather made for a pleasant afternoon.
Ⓒ She showed consideration for my feelings.
Ⓓ He is compassionate about racing cars.

Name_____ Date_____

4. **Which sentence uses an antonym of *ferocious*?**

   Ⓐ The story closed with a grim reality.

   Ⓑ The dog showed me how tame he was by licking my cheek.

   Ⓒ The sounds and sights of the haunted house were frightening to us.

   Ⓓ The bully relentlessly picked on the young boy in the hallway.

5. **Which sentence does not use the second definition of *ferocious*?**

   Ⓐ I woke up with a ferocious headache.

   Ⓑ The ferocious winds blew threw the desert causing a sandstorm.

   Ⓒ The last few weeks of summer brought forth a ferocious heat wave and everyone was advised to stay indoors.

   Ⓓ The dog was tiny, but it was a ferocious animal.

6. **Which sentence uses *ferocious* or either of its derivatives incorrectly?**

   Ⓐ The tiger ferociously tore through the jungle.

   Ⓑ Her ferociously attitude was daunting to the other competitors in the competition.

   Ⓒ The creature's ferociousness was evident by its bared teeth and sharp claws.

   Ⓓ The competition among the students for the student council position was ferocious.

COMMON CORE
STATE STANDARDS

L.6.4–
L.6.6

Name_____ Date_____

Read the passage. Then answer the questions that follow.

My Uncle Gabe sometimes wishes he were a wealthy philanthropist. He is the most genarous soul I know of, and he cares about everyone, even total strangers. He doesn't have a lot of money to donate to charity. But that doesn't stop him from giving.

A few years ago, Gabe gave away his car. He heard about a family with children who didn't have a car or bus service. No one in their right mind would take a taxi every day. Uncle Gabe gave them his car. It was old but reliable, and he said he could take the bus to work. He started saving for a new car but decided he didn't need one after all.

He volunteers with so many organizations that I don't know how he keeps track of them. He hands out sandwiches on the street every Sunday. He also supervises a music program at the senior center. He once joined a gym but ended up giving free volleyball lessons to kids while their parents worked out. He's pretty much always goofing around at something.

Last year, Uncle Gabe asked me if I would like to help him with some of his volunteer work. I said yes because I needed community service hours for school. But it turned out to be so **gratifying** that I have kept on doing it. I help younger kids with their homework and sing with the senior citizens. And I myself always get back more energy and happiness than I give.

1. **Based on the context of the paragraph, what does the word** *gratifying* **mean?**

   Ⓐ amazing

   Ⓑ heartbreaking

   Ⓒ relaxing

   Ⓓ satisfying

Name_____ Date_____

2. **Rewrite the following sentence from the passage so it contains consistency and style with the passage:** *He's pretty much always goofing around at something.*

   Ⓐ Gabriel is a dedicated soul.

   Ⓑ What would you expect from a Leo?

   Ⓒ He just can't quit.

   Ⓓ He's quite the devotee.

3. **Rewrite the following sentence from the passage so it contains a consistent tone with the passage:** *No one in their right mind would take a taxi every day.*

   Ⓐ Taxis were too expensive.

   Ⓑ They totally couldn't afford a taxi.

   Ⓒ It was shameful what taxis charged.

   Ⓓ The price of taxi rides was hilarious.

4. **Which sentence from the passage uses an intensive pronoun?**

   Ⓐ He started saving for a new car but decided he didn't need one after all.

   Ⓑ But that doesn't stop him from giving.

   Ⓒ It was old but reliable, and he said he could take the bus to work.

   Ⓓ And I myself always get back more energy and happiness than I give.

5. **Which of the following sentences or phrases contains a spelling error?**

   Ⓐ He also supervises a music program at the senior center.

   Ⓑ He is the most genarous soul I know of.

   Ⓒ It was old but reliable, and he said he could take the bus to work.

   Ⓓ He doesn't have a lot of money to donate to charity.

COMMON CORE
STATE STANDARDS

L.6.4–
L.6.6

Name_____ Date_____

Read the passage. Then answer the questions that follow.

Cicadas are a type of insect best known for their unique life cycle and the extraordinary amount of noise they make. Typically, however, cicadas are an often misunderstood animal that people think they understand far better than they actually do.

The life cycle of a cicada begins when an adult female cicada lays eggs in the stem of a plant. Eventually, wingless cicadas called nymphs hatch from these eggs and fall to the ground. Once there, they dig in and remain there **perpetually** for up to 17 years. While in the nymph stage, cicadas seek out tree roots and feed on the sap they hold. Unfortunately, this can sometimes **diminish** the health of trees in an area with a high number of nymph cicadas. When the cicadas reach adulthood and are finally ready to emerge from their **subterranean** homes, they crawl to the surface and shed their skin.

People often imagine the emergence of the cicadas to be like a **torrent** of insects flowing out of the Earth, but it's really not that dramatic. While all of the cicadas in the same life cycle do come out at about the same time, there usually aren't enough of them all in one place to cause much of a ruckus. Also, since cicadas are dangerous or destructive, their arrival really isn't like a **plague** taking over the Earth.

1. **Based on context found in this sentence, what does *perpetually* mean?**

Ⓐ seriously

Ⓑ constantly

Ⓒ quietly

Ⓓ peacefully

Common Core
State Standards
L.6.4–
L.6.6

Name_____ Date_____

2. Using a dictionary, find the definition of *diminish* as used in the passage.

Ⓐ to make less

Ⓑ to lessen the authority of

Ⓒ to shrink

Ⓓ to belittle

3. Based on what you know about Greek and Latin roots and affixes, what is the meaning of *subterranean*?

Ⓐ in the dark

Ⓑ temporary

Ⓒ underground

Ⓓ made of dirt

4. Which of these words is a synonym of *torrent*?

Ⓐ trickle

Ⓑ gang

Ⓒ army

Ⓓ flood

5. Using a dictionary or other reference material, what part of speech is the word *plague*?

Ⓐ noun

Ⓑ verb

Ⓒ adjective

Ⓓ preposition

Name_____ Date_____

Read the passage. Then answer the questions that follow.

Bread is a food made using flour and water. People all around the world eat bread, but it may look very different in different places. Bread may be flat, round, long, or braided. It might contain fruits or meats. However people **produce** it, bread has been important in the history of many cultures.

The types of bread made in different parts of the world are usually based on the kinds of grain grown there. Corn, **rye**, oats, and wheat may be ground to make flour. Long ago, before people learned to farm, they had to gather wild grains to make flour. They used the types of grains that grew where they were. At first, people cooked bread on hot rocks. Most bread was flat because people didn't know how to make it rise. Over time, people learned to use yeast. Yeast makes dough puff up **like a balloon**.

Some types of bread haven't changed much over time. Tortillas are flat breads made of ground corn or wheat. Tortillas, which are common in Mexico, may be wrapped around fillings such as meat, beans, and cheese. Another type of flat bread, naan, has been made in central Asia for thousands of years. Light and airy naan is made with wheat flour. It is usually baked in a special oven that makes it puff up quickly. Naan is similar to pita bread. Both naan and pita can be used as wraps or to scoop up other foods. Even pizza, beneath its **flavorful** blanket of cheese and sauce, is bread.

1. **What is the meaning of the word *produce* as used in the passage?**

   Ⓐ fruits and vegetables

   Ⓑ organize

   Ⓒ present

   Ⓓ make

Name_____ Date_____

2. What kind of figure of speech does the expression *like a balloon* represent?

Ⓐ personification

Ⓑ metaphor

Ⓒ simile

Ⓓ irony

3. What does the underlined portion of the passage mean?

Ⓐ Cheese and sauce keep pizza from getting cold.

Ⓑ Cheese and sauce are layered on pizza.

Ⓒ Pizza is very hot.

Ⓓ Pizza is colorful.

4. What is rye?

Ⓐ a type of corn

Ⓑ a kind of bread

Ⓒ a type of grain

Ⓓ a kind of baking

5. Which word provides a connotation similar to *flavorful*?

Ⓐ revolting

Ⓑ repellent

Ⓒ appetizing

Ⓓ nauseating

Answer Key pages 7—19
Practice Answer Key

page 7

1. I   2. they   3. he
4. I, we   5. you   6. they

page 8

1. he   2. she   3. they
4. I, we   5. you, it
6. she
7. they   8. you

page 9

1. me   2. me, it, her   3. them
4. him, us   5. them   6. me
7. me   8. us

page 10

1. me   2. her   3. him
4. them   5. us   6. you
7. him   8. me, them

page 11

1. Her dog ate her brand new purse when he was left alone.
2. Their biology teacher asked Ralph and Bernito to hand in their assignments.
3. Jorge put his coat and books in his locker at school.
4. This picture is our favorite.

page 12

1. a   2. b   3. a
4. b   5. b   6. a

page 13

(sample answers shown)

My (possessive) friends Bart and Amy and I (subjective) love to go geo-caching. They (subjective) often call me (objective) on Saturday mornings to see if I (subjective) can go out with them (objective). Their (possessive) dad usually drives us (objective). Sometimes we (subjective) use my (possessive) GPS, and sometimes we (subjective) use theirs (possessive). We (subjective) usually find amazing treasures!

page 15

1. herself   2. himself
3. ourselves   4. themselves
5. themselves   6. herself
7. himself   8. myself

page 16

1. herself   2. myself
3. ourselves   4. itself
5. himself   6. yourselves
7. themselves   8. yourself

page 17

1. b   2. a   3. a
4. b   5. b   6. b

page 19

1. themselves; itself
2. our, we; its, it
3. she; it
4. him, you; her, she
5. your; their

Common Core Language Grade 6 • ©2014 Newmark Learning, LLC

Answer Key pages 20—28

page 20

1. we
2. him
3. its, it
4. their
5. you
6. her
7. your, you
8. myself

page 21

1. his or her
2. its
3. himself
4. its
5. they, their
6. it
7. their
8. herself
9. our, ourselves
10. she

page 23

1. it
2. his
3. it
4. he
5. they
6. she/her
7. it
8. them

page 24

(sample answers shown)

1. they; After Wendy and Matt took the dogs to the park, the dogs didn't want to go home.
2. it; The ball bounced off the rim, and it broke the backboard.
3. he; Reggie called his friend, but his friend never answered the phone.
4. they; The teachers said the students were going to visit a museum.
5. it; Take the top off the box, and hand the box to me.

page 25

(sample answers shown)

1. she/her (a) Maureen promised her mom that she would clean her own room.

(page 25 continued)

(b) Maureen told her mom, "I promise to clean my room."

2. it (a) The decision to quit his job came as a big surprise to his family. (b) His family was surprised by his decision to quit his job.

3. it (a) The teacher's decision to cancel recess upset the students. (b) The students were upset by the teacher's decision to cancel recess.

4. he/his (a) After Mario graduated, he tossed his hat into the air as Arnold congratulated him. (b) Arnold congratulated Mario for graduating, and Mario tossed his hat into the air.

page 27

1. in
2. their
3. lingered
4. kicks
5. himself
6. high

page 28

(sample answers shown)

Dear City Councilman,

I am writing this letter to inform you of an incident concerning my neighbor and me. An old tree on my neighbor's property hangs over my property. My neighbor does not maintain the tree, and its limbs and leaves fall into my pristine yard.

I asked my neighbor to trim the limbs, but he refuses. I even offered to share the cost of having the tree maintained. He still will not budge.

Is there anything that the city can do to help me?

Sincerely,

Shirley Jones

Answer Key pages 29—35

page 29

1. blew
2. clumsily
3. their
4. myself, relax
5. committed
6. down
7. shined
8. smile, their
9. from
10. us, our

page 30

(sample answers shown)

1. Maria's sister Gretchen works/worked as an aide in a veterinary hospital.
2. After the class is over, the students return their materials to the teacher.
3. The couple danced gracefully to the music.
4. Ernesto refused to take an umbrella with him on the trip to the park.
5. The team won the playoff game and made it to the finals.
6. The three brothers walk/walked from their house to the field to play baseball.

page 31

(sample answers shown)

Photography is more than just snapping pictures of random objects or people. It's an art form and takes lots of practice. You need the right light, angle, and subject to capture the perfect shot. Take your camera with you everywhere you go, so you don't miss out on a perfect shot.

Go outdoors and explore nature. Take advantage of the natural light that the environment offers. Capture brilliant flowers against a sunlit sky. Don't be afraid of a little rain or cloudy skies. Gray or white clouds provide the perfect background for snapping shots of birds and squirrels.

page 33

1. My brother, whom I miss terribly, is away at college.
2. The fortieth president of the United States, Ronald Reagan, was also an actor.
3. The locksmith used a slim-jim, a thin strip of metal used to open locks, to pry open the car door.
4. Janie went to see a podiatrist, a foot doctor, because she felt pain in her heel.
5. Matt, who was late to school again, rushed to get dressed and darted out the door.
6. Mr. Bowie, who is a member of the British Historical Society, will be the speaker at our next meeting.

page 34

(sample answers shown)

1. Uncle Todd's truck, a black 2010 model, needs new tires.
2. The waiters set up the tables and chairs, which were needed for the meal.
3. Jane Austen, an English novelist, wrote the book *Pride and Prejudice.*
4. My favorite restaurant, Sal's Pizzeria, serves pizza and hoagies.
5. The Washington Monument was named after George Washington, the first president of the United States.

page 35

1. J. K. Rowling's *Harry Potter and the Sorcerer's Stone* (1997) was the first book in the Harry Potter series.
2. Astronauts Neil Armstrong and Buzz Aldrin were part of the first mission (July 20, 1969) to the moon.

Answer Key pages 35—39

Answer Key

(page 35 continued)

3. Martin Luther King Jr. is best known for a speech ("I Have a Dream") that he gave during the March on Washington for Jobs and Freedom in 1963.

4. In 1920 women were granted the right to vote with the addition of an amendment (Nineteenth Amendment) to the Constitution.

5. My mom cooked us spaghetti and meatballs (my favorite) for dinner.

page 36

(sample answers shown)

1. My neighbor's dog (a Jack Russell terrier) can jump almost as high as the fence in the yard.

2. Mark Twain (1835–1910) wrote *The Adventures of Tom Sawyer.*

3. Nina is not allowed to have a pet (even though she really wants one) because she has allergies.

4. Tickets for the event will be available until the day of the event (or until they are all sold).

5. *The Wizard of Oz* (my favorite movie) is the story of a girl named Dorothy who gets lost in the land of Oz with her dog, Toto.

page 37

1. Her choices in different cuisines— from Thai to Indian—show her willingness to try new things.

2. The brothers—Guillermo, Marco, Roberto, and Julio—all played on the football team during high school.

3. Her mother—a Girl Scout leader, a coach, and a full-time dentist—does not have enough time to participate in the annual bake sale.

(page 37 continued)

4. Margaret Thatcher was the first woman—and the longest-serving— prime minister of the United Kingdom.

5. Heirloom roses grow in many different colors—red, pink, peach, orange, and yellow.

page 38

(sample answers shown)

1. His decision to leave the company was based on one reason—more family time.

2. They learned about different marine animals—starfish, dolphins, whales—in biology class.

3. Amy read the list from the cookbook—vanilla, flour, baking soda, and sugar—and added the ingredients to the bowl.

4. My grandfather enjoys reading the phone book for fun—no joke!

5. She demanded one thing from her students—participation.

page 39

(sample answers shown)

1. Ansel Adams, one of America's most famous nature photographers, is known for his scenic photographs of the American West.

2. A long lens, called a telephoto lens, allows a photographer to take pictures from a distance without being seen or heard.

3. The word *photography* (fuh-TAH-gruh-fee) comes from the Greek language.

4. Many people enjoy photographing nature. (For some people, it's a career.)

Answer Key pages 39—47

(page 39 continued)

5. Nature photographers pay attention to the same things artists do—colors, lines, curves, and layout.

6. Photography can show us how nature looks in far parts of the world—exotic animals, plants from other habitats, and environments that are very different from those in which we live.

page 41

1. accidentally
2. guarantee
3. fascinate
4. attendance
5. foreign
6. occasion
7. judgment
8. necessary
9. privilege
10. separate
11. vacuum
12. noticeable
13. immediately
14. desperately
15. embarrass
16. mischievous
17. physical
18. believe
19. psychic
20. argument

page 42

1. tournament
2. assistance
3. deceived
4. professional
5. illustrated
6. essential
7. numerous
8. accidentally

page 43

1. loose
2. accepted
3. advice
4. bizarre
5. course
6. ensure
7. peddled
8. stationary
9. principal
10. poured

page 45

(sample answers shown)

1. Your brother Steven went to the store to buy you some bread.

2. Michael went to the doctor, and the doctor told him he was sick.

3. Derek smiled as his father threw him the baseball.

4. Liz and Megan are sisters, but Liz has always been taller than Megan.

page 46

(sample answers shown)

1. (a) The greatest thing that happened at the game was when I caught the fly ball. (b) An amazing thing happened at the game today—I caught the fly ball!

2. (a) I bet it's amazing to go into space. (b) If I ever had a chance to go into space, I bet it would be amazing.

3. (a) When she sang my favorite song at the concert, I was so excited! (b) I was so excited last night when she sang my favorite song at the concert.

page 47

(sample answers shown)

1. After the duel ended, the knight slowly put away his sword and walked away victorious.

2. "The castle fortress is strong," said the king's adviser. "We'll be able to hold back the army."

3. As the ship sailed through the endless sea, the black flag on the mast billowed in the wind.

4. The two green dragons are best friends; they've known each other since birth.

Answer Key pages 48–55

page 48

(sample answers shown)

1. Last weekend we went to an amusement park a few hours away from my house. It was so much fun, and we rode many rides. I rode roller coasters, the Ferris wheel, and the log ride. At the end of the day, we were exhausted, but it was worth it!

2. My class went to an art museum this week. We spent all day looking at the many paintings. I liked the landscapes best. I saw Monet's painting *Poppies Blooming,* which is my favorite.

page 49

(Sample answer shown)

White Sands National Monument is a United States monument located in New Mexico. Dunes of rare white sand, called gypsum sand, cover 275 square miles of desert. Many species of plants and animals live there. They have adapted in order to survive in the harsh environment, which has extreme weather and very little water.

page 50

(sample answers shown)

1. I was anxious about Friday but I tried to keep calm.

2. I was anxious about Friday, but I tried not to worry.

3. Should I be anxious about Friday?

4. I am anxious about Friday.

5. My mom and I feel anxious about Friday and are trying not to worry.

page 51

Answers will vary.

page 53

(sample answers shown)

1. Someday researchers may find a cure for acne.

2. We'll probably go to the movies soon.

3. For example, after the Civil War, Clara Barton managed the Office of Missing Soldiers.

4. I am extremely concerned about the poor condition of Route 35 in Clark County.

page 54

Answers will vary.

page 55

(sample answers shown)

1. She tried not to be bitter about losing.

2. The old, abandoned house was gloomy and dark.

3. We read a fanciful story about an elf.

4. She is always in a great mood and has such a whimsical sense of humor.

5. His malicious behavior caused him to lose friends.

6. This fruit punch has no natural flavors, only artificial ones.

Answer Key pages 56—67

page 56

(Sample answer shown)

Leonardo da Vinci was one of the most famous Renaissance thinkers ever to live. He was an artist, sculptor, scientist, and inventor. Historians speculate that his favorite ideas and inventions were his flying machines. Da Vinci was fascinated with the idea of flying. He studied animals, especially bats, to understand how they were able to fly.

His actual flying machine probably would have flown, but he wasn't able to get it off the ground. Despite this, da Vinci remains one of the most influential scientists.

page 59

1. guess
2. conversation
3. bent
4. shy
5. story

page 60

absolute, formidable, sponsored, introduced, reject, compose, propose, maintained

page 61

1. a 2. b 3. a
4. b 5. a

page 62

1. b 2. a 3. a
4. a 5. b 6. a

page 63

1 products
2. bombarded
3. brilliant
4. brisk
5. b
6. a
7. b

page 65

(sample answers shown)

1. defrost; In the winter, I let my car warm up while I'm getting ready in order to defrost the windows.
2. nonstick; Use a nonstick baking pan for the cookies.
3. prevent; In order to prevent an accident, we must follow the rules.
4. subway; We aren't traveling very far, so we should take the subway.

page 66

(sample answers shown)

1. likable; Sara is a very kind, polite, and likable person.
2. retirement; After working for 40 years, my parents are entering retirement.
3. justify; If you can justify why this is a good cause, I will donate money.
4. nervous; He was nervous while giving his presentation in front of the class.

page 67

(sample answers shown)

1. interweave; inter-; between; to weave between
2. nonstop; non-; not; without stopping
3. purify; -ify; make; to make pure
4. marvelous; -ous; full of; full of wonder or marvel
5. preexist; pre-; before; to exist before
6. transatlantic; trans-; across; crossing the Atlantic

Answer Key pages 68–73

page 68

1. ab-; not present, away from
2. anti-; against
3. bi; two
4. ex-; to leave or go out
5. inter-; the actions between another person or thing
6. -ible; able
7. -ian/an; a native of Canada
8. -ess; female
9. -ic; having artistic qualities
10. -ify; to make simple

page 69

1. c   2. b
3. a   4. d

page 70

1. react   2. barometers
3. aquarium   4. transport
5. involve

page 71

(sample answers shown)

1. biology; I took biology in college because I wanted to study living organisms.
2. autograph; After the movie premiere, we met the lead actor, and he gave us his autograph.
3. vacant; The house was vacant for a long time.
4. civilian; The Air Force pilot married a civilian, someone not in the military.

page 72

(sample answers shown)

1. a) uniform; The police officer had to wear a uniform to work every day. b) perform; She will perform the song onstage at the school concert.
2. a) unicycle; The unicycle was difficult to ride because it only had one wheel; b) motorcycle; The engine on the motorcycle was very loud!
3. a) transport; The ship was able to transport my car across the ocean. b) portable; Portable speakers are nice because you can take them with you.

page 73

(sample answers shown)

1. In college I played on an intercollegiate soccer team with a neighboring university.
2. Weren't dinosaurs just huge, terrible lizards?
3. I don't know if that cake is edible, so don't eat it yet!
4. In science class, we learned about exothermic reactions, which happen when heat or energy is released.
5. A country governed by a plutocracy, or a wealthy group, wouldn't be very fair or prosperous.

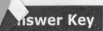

Answer Key pages 74—81

page 74

1. temporary
2. erupt
3. vapid
4. granary
5. defect
6. biannual

page 75

(sample answers shown)

1. mono, lith; In the film *2001: A Space Odyssey*, a giant rectangular monolith is in space.

2. pseudo, nym; The author used a pseudonym for her book because she did not want to use her real name.

3. cen, al; Every one hundred years, our town has a centennial celebration.

4. contra, dict; He never agrees with what I say; he always has to contradict me.

5. dia, log; Writing dialogue between two characters can be very difficult.

page 77

1. knee
2. new
3. mitt
4. bit
5. pie

page 78

(sample answers shown)

1. ˈinvəlid; an injured person made weak or disabled; After the accident, she was considered an invalid because she couldn't walk well.

2. inˈvalid; not valid, false; Your response is an invalid answer to the question I asked.

3. ˈmäd(ə)rət; average in amount; The test was of moderate difficulty, so most people should pass.

4. ˈmädəˌrāt; to preside over a group; She was chosen to moderate the high school debate competition.

page 79

(sample answers shown)

1. adj; small, of less importance

2. noun; a supplementary degree/area of concentration

3. noun; a student with special duties

4. verb; observe or check the quality of

page 80

1. 24 or 25 sheets of paper
2. skiing or sailing
3. a very strong wind
4. argumentative, uncooperative
5. rumbling or gurgling noise from the stomach
6. smelling
7. books printed before 1501
8. quarrel; argument

page 81

1. thesaurus; ineffective, fruitless

2. dictionary; a) *v.* to press or flatten; b) *n.* a fruit with seeds; Do not set the milk on top of the bread or you will squash the loaf!

3. thesaurus; detest, loathe

4. dictionary; ˈemfəˌsīz; My mom made sure to emphasize that my room had to be cleaned by tomorrow.

Answer Key pages 83—89

page 83

(sample answers shown)

1. <u>reluctant</u>: unwilling or hesitant

2. <u>inept</u>: clumsy; having no skill

3. <u>verge</u>: brink; threshold

4. <u>trivial</u>: of little value or importance

page 84

1. allusion   2. illusion   3. capital

4. capitol   5. accept   6. except

page 85

1. a   2. c   3. b   4. d   5. c

6. a   7. c   8. d   9. b   10. d

page 87

(sample answers shown)

1. personification; The writer's computer is not working properly.

2. simile; The baby is so pretty it can be compared to a picture.

3. irony; It's ironic that a car mechanic has car problems because repairing cars is his or her job.

4. metaphor; Just as an engine keeps machines going, the heart keeps a body running.

page 88

1. The angry ocean threw huge waves against the shore.

2. The squirrel enjoyed a take-out dinner of acorns and birdseed.

3. The mailbox opened its mouth and gobbled up the letters.

4. The hateful lightning flashed a warning to the hikers.

5. I looked up at the night sky and saw a star wink at me.

page 88 (continued)

(sample answers shown)

6. The crying child was as loud as a rocket engine.

7. The toy boat sank like a rock.

8. Suzann's pet dog is a cuddly teddy bear.

9. I tried to carry the book bag but it was a sack of bricks.

10. The storm tossed the boat like it was a rag doll.

page 89

1. personification; The noise the rain was making on the roof sounded like someone tap-dancing on it.

2. irony; To study for a Spanish test instead of an English test is ironic because he or she studied the wrong language, and they most likely speak English as their first language.

3. simile; Having a hat taken away evokes a similar response to a hornet being bothered.

4. metaphor; The cars and people on the streets were so small from the sky that they looked like ants on the ground.

5. personification; The flowers are healthy and growing, as if they are happy.

6. simile; Watching paint dry is lengthy and tedious, which is how sitting in the class feels.

Answer Key pages 91—96

page 91
(sample answers shown)
1. My mom's hat blew away, so my brother retrieved it.
2. The little boy was so bashful that he hid behind his father.
3. Sara wants to work for NASA, so she takes many science classes.
4. Because they are strong and hardy, the roses won't die in the harsh winter.
5. Because she refused to apologize to her brother, he still held a grudge.

page 92
1. nighttime
2. crying
3. safety
4. blizzard
5. dusk
6. c 7. a
8. e 9. b
10. d

page 93
1. flower
2. country
3. hour
4. baseball team
5. sentence
6. finger
7. forest
8. pack

page 94
1. lungs
2. second
3. pens
4. ice
5. Canada
(sample answers shown)
6. Bumper is to car as wing is to plane.
7. Cord is to phone as mouse is to computer.
8. Bulb is to lamp as blinds are to window.

page 95
1. dance
2. clothes
3. fruit
4. meat
5. wood
6. musical instruments

page 96
1. flowers
2. cloth
3. literature
4. dessert
5. e
6. a
7. f
8. b
9. c
10. d

136

Common Core Language Grade 6 • ©2014 Newmark Learning, LLC

Answer Key pages 97—101

page 97

1. item/category
2. cause/effect
3. cause/effect
4. part/whole
5. part/whole
6. part/whole
7. cause/effect
8. item/category

page 99

(sample answers shown)

1. considerate; positive

   showing deep unhappiness; negative
2. having an effect; neutral

   having need to dominate; negative
5. quick, intelligent; neutral
6. exceptionally clever; positive

page 100

1. positive
2. negative
3. neutral
4. neutral
5. negative

(sample answers shown)

6. positive: Diane always receives great deals because she is economical with her time and money.
7. negative: She is very stingy and rarely gets friends a present for their birthdays.
8. positive: By being frugal, Tom saves a lot of money and always gets the best quality.

page 101

(sample answers shown)

1. Luke expertly tossed the shrimp in garlic and presented it to Rosa on a bed of perfect rice with an arrangement of colorful veggies on the side. Dessert was a rich combination of delicate pastry, roasted nuts, and luscious chocolate.
2. Luke dumped the greasy shrimp onto the plate with overcooked clumps of rice and a wad of wilted greens. Dessert was a combination of undercooked dough, scorched marbles that might once have been nuts, and artificial chocolate syrup.

Answer Key pages 106—114

pages 106–107

1. b

2. c

3. a

4. a

5. c

6. b

pages 108–109

1. b

2. a

3. c

4. a

5. c

6. b

page 110

1. b

2. d

3. a

4. c

5. b

6. a

pages 112–113

1. d

2. b

3. a

4. c

5. c

page 114

(sample answers shown)

Amelia Marin sat down on a bench under a tree in Harris Hill Park. She took a guitar from its case and began to strum softly. Lost in her music, she was surprised to feel something wet touch her hand. Opening her eyes, she saw a large dog sitting on the walkway in front of her. She put out her hand and spoke softly to the animal, but he just looked at her and wagged his tail. Then he bent down and nudged a sturdy stick that lay in front of him. He gave a hopeful woof and nudged the stick again.

"Oh, I see. You want me to throw the stick?" asked Amelia. She looked around for someone the dog might have come with. She saw a teenage girl approaching.

"He and I were going to play," Amelia said. She was a little disappointed.

"Well, if you throw a stick for Cosmo, you could be here for hours. He never knows when to stop!" said the girl.

Answer Key pages 116—125

pages 116–117

1. c

2. c

3. c

4. a

5. c

6. b

page 118–119

1. a

2. c

3. a

4. b

5. d

6. b

pages 120–121

1. d

2. c

3. a

4. d

5. b

pages 122–123

1. b

2. a

3. c

4. d

5. a

pages 124–125

1. d

2. c

3. b

4. c

5. c

Notes

_____

_____

_____

_____

_____

_____

_____

_____

_____

_____

_____

_____

_____

_____

_____

_____

_____

Notes

_____

_____

_____

_____

_____

_____

_____

_____

_____

_____

_____

_____

_____

_____

_____

_____

Notes

Notes

_____

_____

_____

_____

_____

_____

_____

_____

_____

_____

_____

_____

_____

_____

_____

_____

_____

Notes

_____

_____

_____

_____

_____

_____

_____

_____

_____

_____

_____

_____

_____

_____

_____

_____